CDs, Super Glue, and Salsa

series 3

HOW EVERYDAY PRODUCTS ARE MADE

CDs, Super Glue, and Salsa

series 3

HOW EVERYDAY PRODUCTS ARE MADE

Volume 2: H-Z

Mei Ling Rein, Editor

Allison McNeill, Project Editor

REF TS 146 .C37 2003 v.2

CDs, super glue, and salsa

Detroit • New York • San Diego • San Francisco • Cleveland • New Haven, Conn. • Waterville, Maine • London • Munich

THOMSON

━━━★━━━ ™

GALE

CDs, Super Glue, and Salsa, Series 3

Mei Ling Rein, Editor

Project Editor
Allison McNeill

Permissions
Margaret Chamberlain

Imaging and Multimedia
Dean Dauphinais, Christine O'Bryan, Dan Newell

Product Design
Mark Howell, Cynthia Baldwin

Composition
Evi Seoud

Manufacturing
Rita Wimberley

LIBRARY OF CONGRESS CATALOGING-IN-PUBLICATION DATA

CD's, super glue, and salsa : how everyday products are made: series 3 / Mei Ling Rein, editor.

    p. cm.

    Summary: Thirty entries describe the history and manufacturing process of such products as M&M's, spacesuits, and air conditioners, including their design, raw materials, quality control, and future enhancements.

    Includes bibliographical references and index.

    ISBN 0-7876-6476-6 (set) – ISBN 0-7876-6477-4 (v. 1) – ISBN 0-7876-6478-2 (v. 2)
    1. Manufactures–History–Juvenile literature. [1. Manufactures.] I. Rein, Mei Ling.
TS146.C37 2002
670–dc21

2002011307

Contents

Reader's Guide

CDs, Super Glue, and Salsa: How Everyday Products Are Made, Series 3, answers all the questions about the manufacturing of thirty products students use, see, hear about, or read about every day. From common items like ballpoint pens and DVD players, to the less-common, like gas masks and spacesuits, entries describe in vivid detail the whys and hows of the inventions, provide step-by-step descriptions of the manufacturing processes, and even offer predictions about product enhancements for the future.

CDs, Super Glue, and Salsa's photos, illustrations, and lively, fun-to-read language make it easy to understand the sometimes complicated processes involved in creating these everyday products. Use Series 3 along with Series 1 and Series 2 for a one-stop guide to the details behind ninety of today's most fascinating products.

Format

CDs, Super Glue, and Salsa entries are arranged alphabetically across two volumes. In each entry, students will learn the secrets behind the manufacture of a product through the details of its history, including who invented it and why; how it was developed and how it works; how and from what it is made; how the product might be used in the future; and a list of books, periodicals, and Web sites that offer additional information.

Entry subheads make it easy for students to scan entries for just the information they need. Entries include sections that feature the following information:

- Background of product, including details on its history or development
- Raw materials needed for production
- Design of product and how it works
- Manufacturing process
- Quality control
- Future products
- For More Information

Additional Features

The many sidebars present entertaining and interesting facts that pertain to each product. A glossary of product-specific terms runs in the margin of each entry defining difficult terms. The uses and manufacturing processes of each product are enlivened with ninety-four photos and fifty-five illustrations. Each volume includes a general subject index, including entries from Series 1 and Series 2, that provides easy access to entries by listing important terms, processes, materials, and people.

Comments and Suggestions

We welcome comments on this work as well as suggestions for other products to be featured in future editions of *CDs, Super Glue, and Salsa*. Please write: Editors, *CDs, Super Glue, and Salsa*, U•X•L, 27500 Drake Road, Farmington Hills, Michigan, 48331-3535; call toll-free: 1-800-877-4253; fax to 248-699-8097; or send e-mail via http://www.gale.com.

Hair Dye

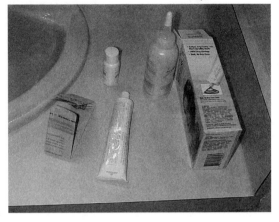

Hair dye is a product that changes the color or tone of hair. Each year, hair coloring products account for $7 billion of the $37 billion hair-care industry earnings worldwide. Sales in the United States make up over $1 billion of these earnings. The percentage of American women who color their hair grew from about 7 percent in 1950 to more than 75 percent in 2001. This proportion is expected to increase as the baby boomers (people born between 1946 to 1964) turn gray. In addition, more and more men are coloring their hair, representing more than $113 million in home-use sales in 2001. Manufacturers are also attracting the younger population, especially teenagers who are using hair color as a fashion accessory.

In the United States, the percentage of women who color their hair grew from about 7 percent in 1950 to more than 75 percent in 2001.

Early hair dyes

People have used hair dyes since ancient times. Records of ancient Egyptians, Greeks, Hebrews, Persians, Chinese, and early Hindus mention the use of hair coloring. The ancient Egyptians did not care for gray hair and developed different methods to cover it. The orange-red dye obtained from the leaves of the henna shrub was a popular hair coloring rinse. Both men and women experimented with different colors, including blue, green, gold, and red. Mummies have even been found with dyed hair.

Ancient Persians also used henna to color not only their hair and beards but also their faces. Ancient Greek women dyed their hair blue and sprinkled it with colored powder, while the men dyed theirs red to show courage. Ancient Romans used the mineral calcium oxide, or quicklime, to achieve a red-gold hair color. To change gray hair to a dark brown color, they used walnut oil made from walnut shells soaked in olive oil.

Before the invention of modern dyes, Europeans and Asians used different plant extracts for hair dyes. Indigo, a fabric dye, was combined with henna to produce light brown to black shades. An extract of chamomile flowers used to lighten hair color is still used in many hair preparations today. Hair dye was also obtained from the wood of some trees—brown dye from the brazilwood tree and yellow dye from the fustic, a tree in the mulberry family. Some of these plant-derived dyes were mixed with metal, such as copper and iron, to produce longer lasting or richer shades.

Metallic salts, powders, and crayons

During the Renaissance (fourteenth through sixteenth centuries), Italian women produced the popular golden red coloring by combing a solution of rock alum, black sulfur, and honey through their hair and then drying it in sunlight until they had achieved the desired shade. Other hair dyes dating back to the sixteenth century included preparations of lead, quicklime, and salt, or silver nitrate and rose water.

During the seventeenth and eighteenth centuries in Europe, pure white powder for hair or wigs was a sign of aristocracy. White powder was made of wheat starch or potato starch, sometimes mixed with plaster of Paris, flour, chalk, or burnt alabaster (a white mineral used for agriculture). Powdered wigs were especially popular among men.

Some experimented with colored powders, made by adding natural pigments to white powder. For example, to make brown powder, burnt sienna or umber, each a type of soil containing iron or manganese oxide, was mixed with white powder. A black ink called India ink was used to make black powder. Some people bleached their hair with lye, which made it fall out.

Other hair colorants were made from wax, soap, and pigments formed into crayon-like blocks. The block was dampened and rubbed on the hair, or applied with a wet brush. These natural substances remained the sources of hair dyes until the nineteenth century. During the mid-nineteenth century, powdered gold and silver became a fad. This was a throwback to biblical times, when people used powdered gold on their hair.

antioxidant: A substance that prevents the hair dye from reacting with the oxygen in the air.

demipermanent hair dye: Does not contain ammonia so it does not lighten the hair. However, it contains a small quantity of peroxide and lasts about twenty-four to twenty-six shampoos.

melanin: The natural pigment of the hair.

permanent hair dye: Works by lightening the hair's melanin, or natural pigment, and then coloring it.

pH: A measure of the acidity of a liquid or solution.

pigment: A natural substance occurring in, and giving color to, a plant or animal.

Modern hair dyes

French chemist Louis-Jacques Thenard (1777–1857) discovered hydrogen peroxide, a compound of hydrogen and oxygen, in 1818, but it was not until 1867 that its use as a hair lightener was recognized. During the 1880s, the amino dyes were developed and marketed in Europe. In 1907, French chemist Eugene Schueller (1881–1957) created the first safe commercial hair color formula, which he called *Auréole*. The formula, based on a new chemical, paraphenylenediamine, led to the foundation of the French Harmless Hair Dye Company, now popularly known as L'Oréal.

The 1950s saw the growing popularity of home-use hair coloring products. The introduction of semipermanent colors further spurred their sales. In the 1980s, the demipermanent products were introduced. They lasted longer than semipermanent colors.

So many choices

Hair dye products come in three basic categories—Level 1 (semipermanent color), Level 2 (demipermanent color), and Level 3 (permanent color). A semipermanent dye does not lighten the hair because it does not contain peroxide or ammonia. It does not interact with the hair's natural pigment and imparts color by coating the hair. It covers just 50 percent of gray hair and generally lasts about six to twelve shampoos. A demipermanent dye does not contain ammonia so it does not lighten the hair. However, it contains a small quantity of peroxide and lasts about twenty-four to twenty-six shampoos.

Permanent hair dyes are the most popular of the three basic types of hair dyes because the color lasts until the person's natural hair color begins to grow in. They work by lightening the hair's melanin, or natural pigment, and then coloring it. There are two types of permanent hair dyes—the oxidation hair dye and the progressive hair dye. Oxidation hair dye products contain a solution of hydrogen peroxide (the developer) and an ammonia solution of dye intermediaries and preformed dyes (the couplers). The dye intermediaries undergo a chemical reaction to form color, while the preformed dyes aid in achieving the desired shade. The second type of permanent dye is the progressive hair dye, which is typically used by men. Progressive hair dyes are applied over a period of time and change hair color gradually. Lead acetate, a color additive, is generally the active ingredient used in these hair dyes. Although the U.S Food and Drug Administration (FDA) has approved lead acetate (0.6 percent concentration) for progressive hair dyes, there are questions about its absorp-

semipermanent hair dye: Does not lighten the hair because it does not contain peroxide or ammonia. Imparts color by coating the hair. It generally lasts about six to twelve shampoos.

•The same permanent hair dye may produce different results in different users. This is because the product works with the hair's natural pigment, called melanin, as the color base. Before permanent color can be applied on the hair, hydrogen peroxide has to first break the melanin down to an almost colorless liquid that then drips out of the hair. Only after the person's natural hair color has been removed can the dye work on the hair. The resulting color is, therefore, a combination of the lightened natural pigment and the added dye color.

•Hair color instructions tell consumers that hair color should be applied to clean "unshampooed" hair. Applying hair color right after shampooing can increase the sensitivity of the scalp, because shampooing removes or reduces the natural oils that protect the scalp during the coloring process. The natural oils in hair also help color to cling to strands.

tion into the body. To play it safe, many men have switched to women's hair dyes for color changes.

Raw Materials

Most commercial hair dye formulas are complex, produced from dozens of ingredients. Moreover, the formulas differ from manufacturer to manufacturer. Hair dyes are generally made from dyes, modifiers, antioxidants, alkalizers, soaps, ammonia, wetting agents, and fragrance.

Hair dyes also contain small amounts of chemicals that give hair a certain characteristic (such as a softer texture) or give a desired action to the dye (such as making it more or less permanent). The chemicals used are usually amino compounds and are listed on the product ingredient list with such names as 4-amino-2-hydroxytoluene and m-Aminophenol. Metal oxides that are used as pigments include titanium dioxide and iron oxide.

Modifiers are chemicals that stabilize the dye pigments or modify (make slight changes to) the shade. Modifiers may bring out a color tone, such as green or purple, which complements the dye pigment. Resorcinol is a commonly used modifier. Antioxidants prevent the dye from reacting with the oxygen in air. Sodium sulfite is the antioxidant most commonly used. Alkalizers are added to change the pH (acidity) of the dye formula because the dyes work best in a highly alkaline formula. The alkalizer ammonium hydroxide is commonly used.

In addition to the basic ingredients above, a manufacturer may add other substances to the formula to give the product characteristics that distinguish it from other products in the market. These include fragrances and shampoos, as well as ingredients that make the product foamy, creamy, or thick.

Demipermanent and permanent hair dyes are typically packaged with a developer, which is in a separate bottle. The developer generally has a hydrogen peroxide base, with small amounts of other chemicals.

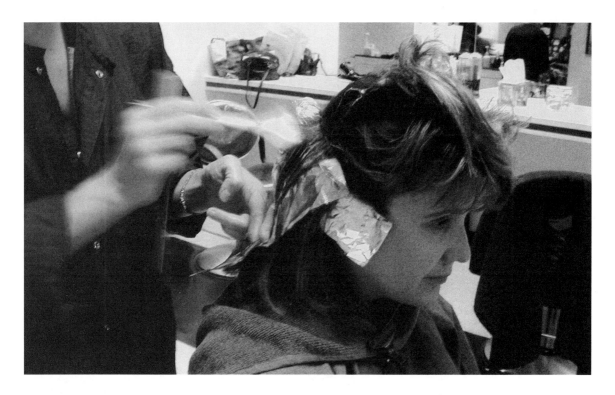

A patron at Maximilian's Salon in Troy, Michigan, has her hair permanently colored by a stylist. The color will eventually grow out as the hair grows, but will not wash out. *Photograph by Kelly A. Quin. Copyright © Kelly A. Quin. Reproduced by permission of the photographer.*

The developer starts the chemical process that brings out the color of the hair dye. It also allows the hair color to last longer.

The Manufacturing Process

Although the formulas for hair dye may differ from manufacturer to manufacturer, the basic production steps are similar.

Checking the ingredients

1 Before a batch of hair dye is made, the chemicals are tested to ensure they are what they are labeled and they are of the correct strength. This process is called certification and may be performed by the manufacturer in-house. In many cases, the ingredients arrive with a Certificate of Analysis from a reputable distributor, and this certification satisfies the manufacturer's requirements.

Much less expensive and quicker than going to a salon, hair coloring has been made convenient with the variety of hair dyes that can be bought at local drugstores and supermarkets. *Photograph by Kelly A. Quin. Copyright © Kelly A. Quin. Reproduced by permission of the photographer.*

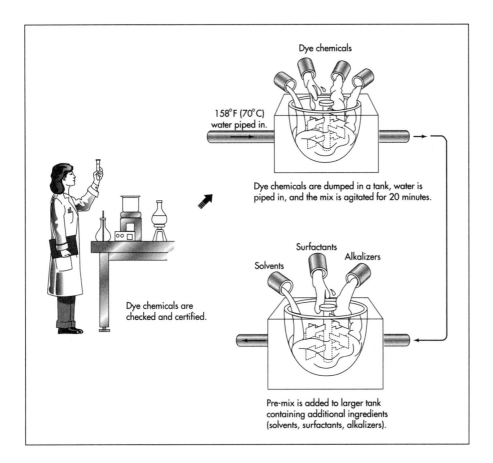

Dye chemicals

158°F (70°C) water piped in.

Dye chemicals are dumped in a tank, water is piped in, and the mix is agitated for 20 minutes.

Dye chemicals are checked and certified.

Surfactants

Solvents   Alkalizers

Pre-mix is added to larger tank containing additional ingredients (solvents, surfactants, alkalizers).

Weighing

2 A worker weighs out the ingredients for a batch. If several ingredients are needed in large amounts, they may be piped in from storage tanks.

Premixing

3 For some hair dye formulas, the dye chemicals are premixed in hot water. The dyes are put in a tank and hot water (158 degrees Fahrenheit or 70 degrees Celsius) is piped in. Other ingredients may also be added to the premix, which is stirred for about twenty minutes.

Mixing

4 Next, the premix is added to a larger tank that contains the rest of the ingredients. If a small batch is being prepared, the portable (movable) tanks used may hold about 1,600 pounds (725 kilograms) of

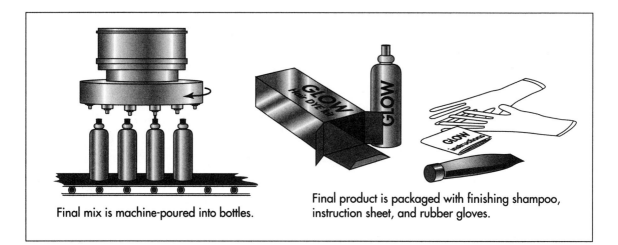

Final mix is machine-poured into bottles.

Final product is packaged with finishing shampoo, instruction sheet, and rubber gloves.

ingredients. A worker wheels the premix tank to the second tank and pours the ingredients. If a large batch is being prepared, the tanks may hold ten times as much as the portable tanks. In this case, the two tanks are connected by pipes. For hair dye formulas that require no premixing, the ingredients are mixed in a tank until the proper consistency is reached.

In some cases, certain ingredients in the second mix are not added during the mixing process. After the hot premix and most of the other ingredients are blended in the second tank, the resulting mixture is allowed to cool. For example, alcohol is not added until the combined mixture is cooled down to 104 degrees Fahrenheit (40 degrees Celsius) because it tends to evaporate at a higher temperature. Fragrances are also added at the end of the mixing process.

Filling

5 The finished batch of hair dye is delivered or piped to a tank with a nozzle in the filling area. Bottles moving on a conveyor belt are filled with measured amounts of the hair dye. The bottles then move on to machines that seal them with caps and affix labels.

Packaging

6 From the filling area, the bottles are taken to the packaging line. The hair dye bottle is put in a box. Other items are added to the box, including a developer, special finishing shampoo, instruction sheet, gloves, and cap. Completed packages are put into shipping cartons, which are taken to the warehouse for distribution.

Quality Control

Although the FDA controls what ingredients may be used in hair dyes, it does not have the authority to require manufacturers to test their products. The FDA is also not authorized to review the results of company testing. Only after consumers have complained about a certain product does the FDA decide if it needs to investigate. The FDA determines if other complaints have been made or if the product has caused serious reactions. If enough evidence shows that the product is harmful, the FDA requests the manufacturer to pull the product from the market.

Reputable manufacturers make sure their researchers test a hair dye formula many times in the laboratory before it reaches the manufacturing stage. They conduct experiments to ensure, among other things, that a formula is non-irritating, works well, and produces the same result each time.

As part of the manufacturing process, workers check their chemicals before they are put into a batch to make sure the correct chemicals with the correct strength are used. After the batch is mixed, samples are taken and subjected to a series of standard tests. Laboratory technicians check the batch for the required viscosity (resistance to flow) and pH (acidity) balance. They also test the batch on a swatch of hair. If the formula is new or if it has been altered, technicians will also test samples of the dye after the filling stage.

The Future

Hair dye manufacturers are increasingly using computers to control and automate the manufacturing process. Computers are used to weigh and measure ingredients, to control chemical reactions, and to regulate equipment, such as pumps. The future may see greater production efficiency as hair dye production becomes fully automated.

In the meantime, manufacturers who test their products continue to do so without having to follow government testing standards. Moreover, the FDA does not see any change in government regulation of hair dyes in the future. As long as manufacturers label their products with such warnings as the possibility of the hair dye causing allergic reactions, they are safe from legal action. Some scientists are conducting research on the possible link of prolonged use of hair dye to the incidence of cancer, and the FDA claims that it is following these studies.

For More Information

Periodicals

Gorman, Jessica. "Chemistry of Color and Curls." *Science News.* (August 25, 2001): pp. 124–126.

Krueger, Diane. "Countdown to Color." *SalonNews.* (September 2001): pp.66–68.

McCann, Lauren. "To Dye for Hair." *Teen Magazine.* (May 2001): pp.89–97.

Meadows, Michelle. "Are Hair Chemicals Safe for You?" *Consumers' Research Magazine.* (March 2001): pp. 19–21.

Web Sites

Cormeny, Sara. "Color-Coded Hair." *Public Broadcasting Service.* http://www.pbs.org/newshour/infocus/fashion/hair.html (accessed on July 22, 2002).

"How Hair Coloring Works." *Marshall Brain's HowStuffWorks.* http:www. howstuffworks.com/hair-coloring.htm (accessed on July 22, 2002).

Raber, Linda. "What's that Stuff?" *Chemical & Engineering News: The Newsmagazine of the Chemical World Online.* http://pubs.acs.org/cen/whatstuff/stuff/7811scit4.html (accessed on July 22, 2002).

Leather Jacket

L eather is a material made from the hide or skin of animals that has been chemically treated. The term "hide" generally refers to the skin of larger animals, such as cows, while the term "skin" is used for smaller animals, such as calves. The term hide is used in this article for all animals.

Since early history, humans have used leather to make clothing. They discovered that after using hunted animals for food, they could wear the hides as protection against cold and bad weather. However, they did not know how to preserve the hides, so that the hides eventually rotted away. Over time, people learned that stretching the hides over frames and then drying them in the sun made them last longer. Later, people learned to clean the animal cells from the hides by scraping them with stones. This method removed the bacteria that caused decay. People also found that hides could be dried with smoke and softened by rubbing with the brains and fats of the animal. Today's leather jackets continue to possess the durability and flexibility that early humans found useful. The timelessness of leather jackets is evident in their popularity among people of all ages all over the world.

Cowhide, antelope hide, lambskin, and buckskin are most commonly used to make leather jackets.

Tannin to the rescue

Evidence indicates that, thousands of years ago, ancient civilizations, including Egypt, India, and China, used a substance called tannin (or tannic acid) found in tree bark to convert animal hides into leather. This process not only preserved the hides but also gave them softness and flexibility. The ancient Hebrews first used the tannin from oak bark, which became the popular source of tannin because it grew in many places. The Greeks discovered that tannin could also be found in walnuts, pomegranate peels, and the bark of conifer trees.

Through the ages

The ancient Phoenicians used leather pipes to transport water from storage containers to their homes. Soldiers of the Roman Empire wore leather shoes and tunics, as well as breastplates and shields. During the Middle Ages (476 C.E.–1453 C.E.), the Moors introduced the softer cordovan leather (named after Córdoba, Spain), which was made from goatskin. Between the 1300s and the 1600s, several guilds (trade associations) within the leather industry had been formed all over Europe. In Central and South America, the Mayan, Incan, and Aztec cultures also used leather, as did the American Indians, who made garments from buckskin, doeskin, and buffalo hide. The American Indians used fish oils for tanning and animal brains and fats for softening hides in much the same manner done by the ancient people.

The Industrial Revolution, which began in England during the second half of the eighteenth century and which swept through the United States during the nineteenth century, resulted in the mechanization of the leather industry. In 1809, Samuel Parker (1779–1866) of Massachusetts invented a machine that split hides to any desired thickness. In the past, if a certain thickness was required, a worker called a currier trimmed the leather, resulting in plenty of wasted material. In 1884, Augustus Schultz, a New York City chemist, developed a tanning method using chromium salts. This method not only cut the tanning process from weeks or months to just hours or days but also made the leather more water-resistant.

Keeping the old, adding the new

Over the years, the manufacture of leather has not changed much. Chrome tanning is the method most used today; however, vegetable tanning is still performed. Although some countries still manufacture leather manually, in the United States computerized programs control machine operations, including the measurement and mixing of chemicals. Interestingly, Parker's splitting machine is still in use.

collagen: The fibrous protein that makes up most of the dermis, or middle layer, of animal hides.

dermis: The thick, middle layer of an animal hide that is processed to obtain leather. Also called corium.

guild: In medieval times, an association of people of the same trade formed for their mutual aid and protection and the setting of standards and regulations.

hoof-and-mouth disease: An infectious viral disease that affects such animals as cattle, sheep, and deer. The animals develop sores in their bodies and become very weak. Some young animals die from the disease.

mad cow disease: A fatal brain disease that causes animals to stagger and behave strangely.

Frequently worn by fighter pilots in World War II (1939–45), leather jackets also became known as bomber jackets.

Raw Materials

Cowhide, antelope hide, lambskin, and buckskin (from male deer and sheep) are most commonly used to make leather jackets. At the meat processing plant, the hide is removed from the animal. (Today, as in the past, animal hides are by-products of the meat industry. Ranchers do not kill cattle just for their hides.) It is immediately refrigerated, salted, or packed in barrels of brine (salt water) to keep it from decomposing. The hide is then sent to the tannery, where it undergoes a series of processes to permanently preserve (prevent decay) and soften it.

Sewing materials, which are typically purchased from outside vendors, are stored in the garment factory. These materials include thread, lining, seam tape, buttons, snaps, and zippers.

The Preparation Process

Before the raw hide can be treated chemically to make it into leather, it has to undergo a thorough cleaning and dehairing. These steps ensure that any decay-causing bacteria are completely destroyed.

mechanization: Using a machine to do work previously done by humans or animals.

production line: A sequence of machines in a factory through which products pass until they are completely assembled.

Trimming and cleaning

1 The hides are trimmed and sorted according to size, weight, and thickness. They are soaked in revolving drums filled with water, detergents, and bactericides (substances that destroy microorganisms). This soaking process removes salt, dirt, and blood, as well as proteins that could encourage the growth of bacteria. Hair is removed using chemical sprays or lime solutions.

2 Excess hair is further scraped off by scudding, a process that removes scuds, or the remaining unwanted hair, dirt, and other substances left in the hair follicle after dehairing. Scudding is done by hand with dull knives or by a machine that squeezes out the scuds. The hides are again washed to remove any remaining chemicals.

3 Next, the hides are soaked in an acid solution. Then, they undergo bating, a process in which they are treated with enzymes, or substances that hasten the breakdown of nonfibrous proteins in the hides. Bating serves to strengthen the collagens (fibrous proteins) in the hide by getting rid of the nonfibrous proteins. This results in soft, flexible hides. Finally, the hides are pickled with salt and sulfuric acid for more softening and cleaning.

Tanning

4 Tanning refers to the process by which hides are preserved and converted into leather. The word is derived from tannin (also called tannic acid), a plant material that bonds the collagen in the dermis of a hide by ridding it of its water content.

One of three methods of tanning may be used. Vegetable tanning consists of soaking the hides in progressively stronger tannic acid solutions for several weeks or months. This method produces a firm leather.

In mineral tanning, the hides are typically soaked in water filled with chromium salt. Since chromium salt is the most frequently used tanning agent, the terms mineral tanning and chrome tanning are often used interchangeably. Aluminum or zirconium salt may also be used. The process, which takes just a few hours or days, produces leather that is softer and more flexible than that made by vegetable tanning.

Oil tanning resembles the ancient methods and uses fish oil that is sprayed onto the hide. The oil is then pounded into the hide. This method was originally used to make leather out of the hide of the chamois, a small antelope native to the mountainous areas of Europe and Asia. Today, chamois leather refers to the soft, absorbent leather made from the inner

suede: The process of raising the fibers on the skin side of a hide to give a velvet nap effect.

tannery: A place where animal skins and hides are converted into leather.

tanning: A chemical process by which animal hides and skins are converted into leather.

side of a sheepskin. It is generally used for polishing and washing.

Washing and drying

5 After tanning, the hides are washed again and wrung out thoroughly to remove all moisture. The hides are passed under a band knife, which cuts the hides horizontally to a uniform thickness. Next, the hides are transported by a conveyor belt to drying tunnels. To prevent shrinkage during drying, the hides are stretched on frames. They are sprayed with water and soap and allowed to hang for a period of time so that the stiffness caused by the drying does not set in.

6 The hides are placed in machines that loosen up the fibers, making the leather more flexible. Finally, the hides are hung in vacuum-drying cabinets.

7 The completely dried hides are buffed with abrasive cylinders. Buffing, a process comparable to sandpapering, is done to remove some surface imperfections. The hides may also be sueded by passing the flesh side of the hides under high-speed emery wheels. This process raises the fibers to produce a velvet nap (fuzzy) effect.

8 The final step is called finishing, or the application of a thin coating on the leather surface to preserve its appearance. Some are glazed for a polished look, while others are dyed, or colored. After the finishing process, the leather pieces are sent to garment factories.

The Manufacturing Process

Leather garments are still considered luxury items, and some consumers are willing to pay more for those that are hand-constructed by skilled craftspeople. The following steps are those used in factory mass production.

Jacket design

1 Garment manufacturers typically employ designers to create patterns from which leather jackets are made. Computerized machines grade the designs based on government tables of body measurements. These tables assign sizes based on body weight and height. The computer then produces patterns using the original design. A variety of pattern sizes are made.

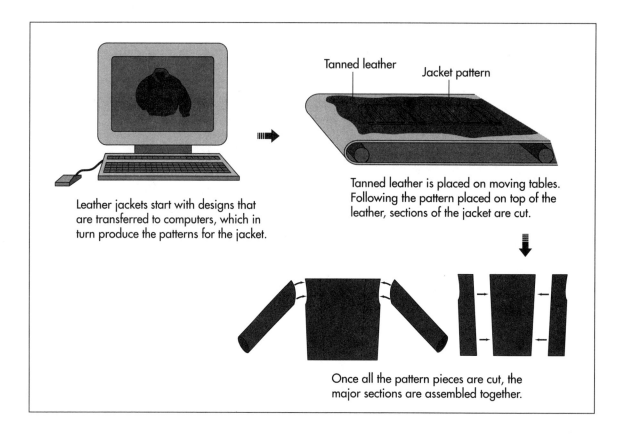

Leather jackets start with designs that are transferred to computers, which in turn produce the patterns for the jacket.

Tanned leather

Jacket pattern

Tanned leather is placed on moving tables. Following the pattern placed on top of the leather, sections of the jacket are cut.

Once all the pattern pieces are cut, the major sections are assembled together.

Cutting

2 The tanned leather is placed on moving tables called spreaders. It is preferable to cut leather one layer at a time. A tissue-paper pattern may be placed on top of the leather, or a pattern is marked on the leather with tailor's chalk. The spreader works like a conveyor belt, moving the leather to the cutting machine. The latest technology uses a computerized laser beam system that vaporizes fabric seams instead of cutting them. The system's high-speed action is ideal for cutting single layers of leather.

3 Lining material for the jacket is cut using the same method. Multiple layers of lining material may be cut at one time.

Jacket assembly

4 The jacket sections are put together. First, the patch pockets are sewn onto the side pieces. The side pieces are then stitched to the back section. Side pockets are sewn in at the same time that the sides

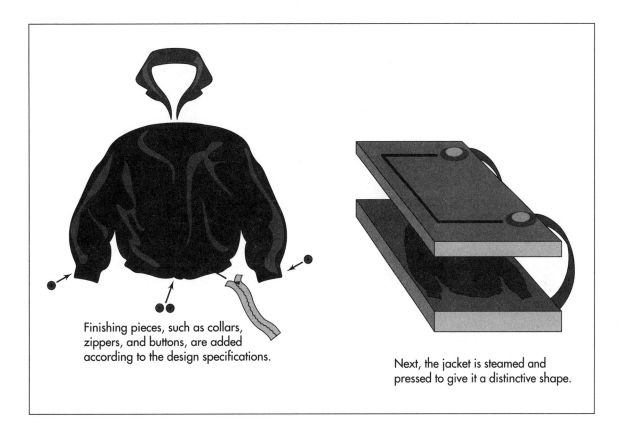

Finishing pieces, such as collars, zippers, and buttons, are added according to the design specifications.

Next, the jacket is steamed and pressed to give it a distinctive shape.

are attached to the back section. The sleeve underseams are sewn together, and then the sleeves are attached to the armholes. The linings are generally assembled before being sewn into the jacket. Buttonholes and finishing pieces, including collars, cuffs, buttonholes, buttons, and zippers, are attached to the jacket according to the design specifications.

The jacket sections and finishing pieces are moved along a production line that uses automatic sewing machines capable of sewing as many as eight thousand stitches a minute. The jacket sections are assembled following sequential steps. For example, a machine sews a cuff to a sleeve, which is then moved to another machine where it is attached to the jacket armhole.

Two machines may work on the jacket at the same time. For example, one machine attaches buttons to the front, while a second machine is adding the collar.

Each step in the jacket assembly is preprogrammed—from setting thread and needle positions to removing the finished product. Devices in the machine automatically knot and cut threads after each seam is sewn.

Leather jackets, often costing thousands of dollars, can be found on the runways of famous fashion designers. *Reproduced by permission of Corbis Corporation.*

Excess threads are removed to trash bins by compressed air.

Although each step of assembling the jacket has been preprogrammed, operators regulate each sewing machine with the help of a presser-foot or a control panel. An operator can stop production to make adjustments, such as to change a broken needle.

Shaping and pressing

5 Finally, different pressing processes involving heat application, steaming, and blocking are performed. To give the jacket a distinctive shape, such as a blazer style or a bomber style, buck presses are used. These presses are equipped with controls and gauges that regulate the amount of steam and pressure. Curved blocks are placed around the collars and cuffs, then heated to achieve a curved effect.

Final inspection

6 Each jacket is inspected by hand before it leaves the factory. The jackets are encased in plastic bags, packed into cartons, and shipped to the sellers.

Quality Control

The tanning process has to be thorough so that the completed product is not only soft and flexible but also free of bacteria-causing proteins that could result in decay. Jacket manufacturers inspect each shipment of leather for marks, tears, stains, and imperfections.

The automatic sewing machines used today are self-correcting. The machines have a display panel like a computer screen. A program within the machine indicates on the display panel any problem in operation, as well as the solution to that problem. The machines have sophisticated lubricating systems (to keep the machines well oiled and working properly), which ensure finished products that are consistently of good quality.

The Future

Despite the high cost of leather, leather jackets continue to be in demand. The new styles and colors have come a long way from the black bike jackets that first became fashionable during World War I (1914–18). Manufacturers have come out with jackets of all colors, including pastels. Lightweight leather jackets for not-so-cold-weather wear and styles that can be worn for different occasions have become very popular. Some manufacturers have produced leather jackets embossed to look like the skins of snakes and alligators. The raised texture characteristic of these more exotic skins is created by heavy pressure of a machine.

DYE JOB

According to experts, to check if a leather jacket has been dyed properly, rub it with a tissue. Very little dye, if any, should come off. This means that the leather was immersed in a dyebath that penetrated the leather, instead of just being superficially sprayed or painted.

For More Information

Books

Scrivano, Sandy. *Sewing with Leather and Suede: A Home Sewer's Guide: Tips, Techniques, Inspirations.* Asheville, NC: Lark Books, 1998.

Periodicals

Donohue, Amy. "Jacket Requirements." *Men's Health.* (October 1997): pp.100-101.

Joyner, Valerie. "The Leather Channel: Warm Temperatures May Be Taking a Toll on Sales, but Outerwear Makers Say Leather Is Saving the Day." *Daily News Record.* (December 17, 2001): p. 145S.

Medintz, Scott. "Leather Report: When a Jacket's Beauty Is Skin Deep." *Money.* (October 1998): pp. 222-223.

M&M's Candy

Photograph by Kelly A. Quin. Copyright © Kelly A. Quin. Reproduced by permission of the photographer.

Over four hundred million M&M's® chocolate candies are produced each day.

The M&M's® chocolate candy is a pellet (small mass) of chocolate encased in a colorful, hard, sugary shell. Some people say that Forrest Mars Sr. (1904–99) got the idea for such a product while in Spain during the Spanish Civil War (1936–1939). He observed how soldiers kept chocolate candies from melting in their pockets by covering the candy with a sugary coating.

Mars wanted to produce chocolate candies that could be sold year-round, especially in the summer when sales usually went down. He put his chocolate candy inside a candy shell, thereby preventing the chocolate from melting. It could be eaten neatly so that, as the ad says, it "melts in your mouth and not in your hand."

Origin of chocolate

At the heart of every M&M's® candy is its chocolate. Chocolate is made from cacao beans, the seeds of the cacao tree, a native plant of South America's river valleys. After being removed from the pods, the beans are dried in the sun to preserve them. The dried beans are called cocoa beans. During the seventh century, the cacao tree was brought to Mexico, where the drink *cacahuatl* (a blend of cocoa beans, red pepper, vanilla, and water) became popular.

In 1528, the explorer Hernán Cortés (1485–1547) took the cocoa drink back to Spain, where the recipe was sweetened using sugar and then heated. For nearly a hundred years, Spain kept secret from other countries its *chocalatal* drink, the ancestor of today's hot chocolate. The Spanish were also the first to eat solid chocolate, although it was nothing like the M&M's® chocolate center. Eventually, in the early 1600s, the sweetened beverage reached Italy. The chocolate drink was introduced to France, following the marriage of the Spanish princess Maria Theresa (1638–1683) to Louis XIV (1638–1715) in 1660. The English started adding milk to the chocolate drink at about 1700. Chocolate candies were also made in Europe in the 1700s, but they were not very popular. The finished products with their crumbly texture did not hold the sugar well. The North American colonists of Dorchester, Massachusetts, first manufactured chocolate in 1765. Their cocoa beans came from the West Indies.

Solid chocolate

In 1828, Conrad van Houten (1801–1887) developed a method to produce the solid chocolate that is known today. The Dutch chocolate maker invented a screw press for squeezing most of the cocoa butter (chocolate fat) out of roasted cocoa beans. The cocoa beans were then ground (reduced to powder form). The ground cocoa was mixed with just enough cocoa butter to make a paste, which was smoother and easier to blend with sugar to produce solid "eating chocolate." About twenty years later, in 1847, an English company called Fry and Sons introduced the first commercially prepared solid eating chocolate.

In 1876, Swiss candymaker Daniel Peter (1836–1919) added dried milk to sweet chocolate to make milk chocolate. In 1913, another Swiss candymaker, Jules Schaud, manufactured chocolate shells filled with other sweets. Although solid sweet chocolates had become quite popular, they were still expensive.

American-made chocolate candies

In the United States, Milton Hershey (1857–1945) used fresh milk to produce chocolate candies in 1904. Using mass production techniques, he

THE SECOND "M" IN M&M'S® CANDY

In 1939, Forrest Mars Sr. approached William Murrie, president of Hershey Chocolate Company (now Hershey Foods Corporation) in Hershey, Pennsylvania, to propose a partnership with Murrie's son, Bruce. The business proposal involved the manufacture of the chocolate candies Mars had recently developed. It would be an 80 percent/20 percent partnership, with Mars owning most of the partnership. It is said that the elder Hershey would provide, among other things, the chocolate that was in scarce supply because of World War II (1939–1945). The Hershey company was making chocolate candies for the American soldiers, and the government did not limit its supply. The new product was named M&M's® after Mars and Murrie.

chocolate liquor:
A thick syrup made from cocoa butter and ground, roasted cocoa nibs, the soft meats of the cocoa bean. The word liquor here does not refer to an alcoholic beverage.

M&M's® candies were packaged in a tube when they were first produced in 1940. *Reproduced by permission of AP/Wide World Photos.*

was able to sell large quantities of individually wrapped chocolate bars at inexpensive prices.

Forrest Mars Sr. first manufactured M&M's® candies in 1940. During World War II (1939–1945), American soldiers carried cardboard tubes of the chocolate candies for snacks. The candies soon became popular with the public. The brown bags now used to package M&M's® candies were first introduced in 1948. The two lower-case "m's" were printed on the candies starting in 1950. The letters, originally in black, were changed to white and remain this color today.

Since its introduction to consumers, the popularity of M&M's® chocolate candies has grown. Several varieties of M&M's® have been introduced over the years, including peanut (1954), almond (1988), mint (1989), and peanut butter (1990). In 1981, the astronauts of the first space shuttle, *Columbia,* chose M&M's® candies to be part of their food supply. In 1987, consumer demand brought back red-colored M&M's® candies, which were discontinued in 1976 because of a health concern related to a particular red food coloring. Although the red coloring was never used in M&M's® candies, the company did not want to confuse consumers. In 1995, more than fifty years after M&M's® candies first came to market, Americans voted to add the color blue to the color mix. Green joined the color mix in 1997. The M&M's®/Mars Company claims that combined sales of all varieties of M&M's candies make it the bestselling snack brand in the United States.

cocoa butter: Chocolate fat.

panning: A process by which the chocolate centers are rotated in large containers, where they are sprayed with liquid candy made of sugar and corn syrup to make a hard candy shell.

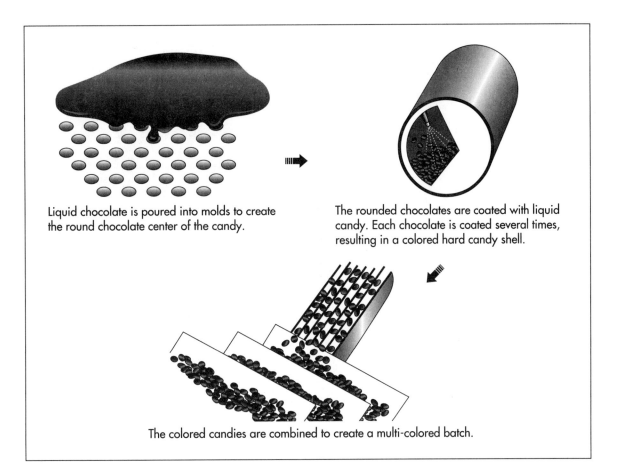

Liquid chocolate is poured into molds to create the round chocolate center of the candy.

The rounded chocolates are coated with liquid candy. Each chocolate is coated several times, resulting in a colored hard candy shell.

The colored candies are combined to create a multi-colored batch.

Raw Materials

M&M's® chocolate candies have two main parts—hardened liquid chocolate and the hard candy shell. Liquid chocolate is a mixture of chocolate liquor, whole milk, cocoa butter, and sugar, among other ingredients. Chocolate liquor is a thick syrup made from cocoa butter and ground, roasted cocoa nibs, the soft meats of the cocoa beans. The second component of an M&M's® chocolate candy is the candy shell made from a mixture of sugar and corn syrup.

The Manufacturing Process

The manufacturing steps that follow are essentially the same for all varieties of M&M's® chocolate candies.

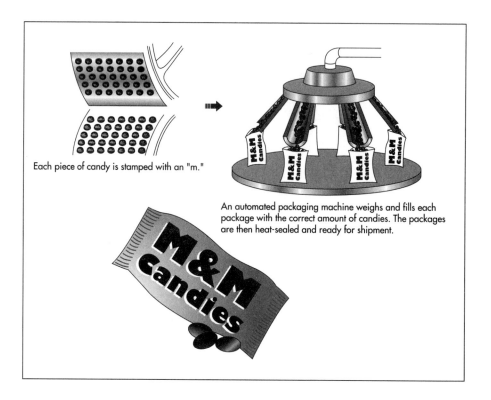

Each piece of candy is stamped with an "m."

An automated packaging machine weighs and fills each package with the correct amount of candies. The packages are then heat-sealed and ready for shipment.

Molding

1 The liquid chocolate is poured into tiny round molds to create the chocolate centers of the candy. For M&M's® Peanut Chocolate Candies or Almond Chocolate Candies, the chocolate surrounds a whole peanut or almond. For M&M's® Peanut Butter Chocolate Candies, the peanut butter center is made first and then surrounded by the chocolate.

2 The formed chocolate pellets are "tumbled" to make them smooth and rounded. They are then allowed to harden.

Coating

3 After the chocolate pellets have become hard, they are moved by conveyor belt to the coating area, where they go through the process called panning.

4 During panning, the chocolate pellets are rotated in large containers, where they are sprayed with liquid candy made of sugar and corn syrup. The spraying is timed in order to allow each coat to

M&M's® are often used to add extra flavor and decoration to recipes such as brownies and cookies. *Photograph by Kelly A. Quin. Copyright © Kelly A. Quin. Reproduced by permission of the photographer.*

dry. In addition, several coats are applied to ensure an even layer of candy coating.

5 Color is added to a finishing syrup, which is applied as the final coat. The final product is allowed to dry to a hardened shell. Each batch of M&M's® chocolate candies is of a different color.

Printing

6 The single-colored batches are mixed to create colorful blends of red, yellow, orange, blue, green, and brown. A special conveyor belt then moves the candies to a machine that stamps the "m" on the

CAST OF CHARACTERS

1940—M&M's® Plain Chocolate Candies were produced for U.S. soldiers for snacks. They were introduced to the American public the following year. The name was changed to M&M's® Milk Chocolate Candies in 2000 because the candies were "just too good to be called 'Plain.' "

1954—M&M's® Peanut Chocolate Candies came in just the color brown when they first hit the market. In 1960, the colors red, yellow, and green were added to the color brown. In 1976, orange was added to the color mix.

1988—M&M's® Almond Chocolate Candies were made available during the Christmas and Easter seasons. However, they were so popular that they were sold year-round starting in 1992.

1990—M&M's® Peanut Butter Chocolate Candies became an instant hit after they first appeared. The peanut butter cream center is surrounded with milk chocolate and encased in the familiar colorful sugar shell.

1995—M&M's® Mini Chocolate Baking Bits are used in every kind of desserts, from cookies to cakes and brownies.

1996—M&M's® Minis Milk Chocolate Candies are smaller in size than the regular M&M's® candies. They come in colorful reclosable plastic tubes. The M&M's® Mega Tubes were added in 2000.

1997—M&M's® Colorworks® Milk Chocolate Candies come in 21 different colors, including pink, maroon, black, silver, and gold. Consumers can choose a blend of colors to represent their companies, schools, or special occasions.

1999—M&M's® Crispy Candies were first sold. Slightly bigger than the regular M&M's® candies, these new additions to the M&M's® family have a crispy rice center surrounded by chocolate and a candy shell.

2001—M&M's® Dulce de Leche-Caramel Chocolate Candies, patterned after a Latin American favorite, caramelized sweetened condensed milk, features a chocolate and caramel swirl inside the candy shell.

shells. Each candy rests in its own shallow hole to keep it in place and is passed under rubber etch rollers that gently print the letter without breaking the candy shell. Over 400 million M&M's® chocolate candies are produced each day.

Packaging

7 A packaging machine weighs the candies, fills each package with the correct number and colors of candies, then heat-seals the package. The colors are distributed based on different proportions. For example, a package of M&M's® Milk Chocolate Candies (referred to as M&M's® Plain Chocolate Candies until the summer of 2000) has 30 per-

cent brown, 20 percent yellow, 20 percent red, 10 percent green, 10 percent orange, and 10 percent blue colors. In comparison, a package of M&M's® Peanut Butter Chocolate Candies has 20 percent each of yellow, red, green, blue, and brown colors.

8 The finished packages are moved along a conveyor belt to a machine that puts together the shipping boxes and fills them with the right number of candy packages. Then, the machine seals the boxes.

Quality Control

Chocolate pieces that are misshapen are removed. However, a candy that is missing the imprinted "m" is not thrown out. Because of very small variations in the shape of the candies, it is not possible for the imprinting process to be perfect.

The Future

Future developments in M&M's® Candy are more likely to occur in colors and additions to the basic chocolate centers. In March 2002, Masterfoods USA, a Mars Inc., company and manufacturer of M&M's® Candy, invited people from seventy-five countries to vote for their favorite new M&M's® Candy color. In June 2002, the company started producing purple M&M's® Candy, which won over aqua and pink.

For More Information

Books

Brenner, Joel G. *The Emperors of Chocolate.* New York, NY: Broadway Books, 2000.

Periodicals

Corzo, Cynthia. "Hispanic M&Ms to hit 5 markets this month." *Knight-Ridder/Tribune News Service.* (July 10, 2001): page K0072.

Web Sites

"About M&M's®." *M&M's® Brand.* http://www.m-ms.com/us/about/index.jsp (accessed July 22, 2002).

"The History of Chocolate." *Chocolate Manufacturers Association.* http://candyusa.org/Chocolate/chocolate.shtml (July 22, 2002).

Magnetic Resonance Imaging Scanner

A computer controls all parts of the MRI scanner. It processes all incoming information and then forms images of the body part being scanned.

A magnetic resonance imaging (MRI) scanner is a machine that uses magnetic fields and radiofrequency (RF) radiation, or radio waves, to take detailed pictures of tissues and organs within the body. MRI is noninvasive, which means that the patient is not subjected to any surgery or X rays. MRI is very valuable in diagnosing (identifying the nature and cause of) disorders of the brain and spinal cord, heart disease, cancers, and injuries and diseases affecting bones, ligaments, and cartilage.

Spinning protons

The MRI scanner was originally called the NMR (nuclear magnetic resonance) scanner. The "nuclear" part of the term was changed in the 1980s because it was feared people might think dangerous radiation was involved in the process. Actually, "nuclear" refers to the nucleus, or the center of an atom.

Under ordinary conditions, components of the nucleus called protons spin around like toy tops. If a powerful, steady magnetic field is applied to the protons, they line up with the magnetic field in an orderly formation. When radio frequency (RF) radiation is directed into the magnetic field, the protons take energy from it and go out of formation. Once the RF signal stops, the protons resume their former positions and emit their own energy, or RF signals, giving away their location. This phenomenon is called nuclear magnetic resonance (NMR).

It is due to NMR phenomenon that magnetic resonance imaging is possible. Each kind of tissue sends out its own characteristic NMR signal. A computer is able to process the signals emitted by the disturbed protons, as well as the time it took them to get back into formation. The computer can also figure out the type of tissue in which the protons are located. It can also search for signals given out by specific types of protons, such as cancer cells. The computer converts this information into three-dimensional pictures on a television screen. Copies of the images are then made.

History

In 1938, American physicist Isidor Isaac Rabi (1898–1988) developed the first basic NMR device, by which he measured the magnetic properties of atoms. He was able to do so by measuring the spin of the protons in the atom's nucleus. Spin refers to the property of the protons that gives them a nuclear magnetic moment, that is, the protons behave like small magnets.

In 1945, two groups of scientists improved on Rabi's NMR device. Many applications of NMR in such fields as biology and chemistry have since resulted from the devices independently developed by Swiss-born Felix Bloch (1905–1983) and his colleagues at Stanford University (California) and the Edward Purcell (1912–1997) research team at Harvard University (Massachusetts).

Two men and a single vision

Raymond V. Damadian (1936–), an American medical doctor and researcher, first proposed the application of NMR in scanning the human body in 1969. In laboratory animal experiments, Damadian found that different body tissues emitted NMR signals that vary in length. He also found that cancerous tissues differ from normal tissues in the quality and length of their NMR signals. In 1977, Damadian and his colleagues, Drs. Larry Minkoff and Michael Goldsmith, formed the first MRI scan of a human being. Actually, Minkoff was the "patient," who had to stay still for nearly five hours during the imaging of his whole body.

At about the same time, British engineer Godfrey Hounsfield (1919–) was also experimenting with nuclear magnetic resonance. Hounsfield had just invented the CAT (computerized axial tomography) scanner, which became commercially available in 1975. Like Damadian,

alloy: A mixture of a metal and a nonmetal or a mixture of two or more metals.

functional imaging: An imaging technique used to determine brain function by relating thought or a body function to certain areas in the brain.

gradient coils: The three magnetic coils located within the main magnet, which are designed to produce desired variations in the main magnetic field to help obtain the three-dimensional information needed for creating precise images of a body part.

nuclear magnetic resonance: A phenomenon in which magnetic fields and radio waves cause the nucleus of an atom to emit small radio signals.

nuclear spin: The property of an atom's nucleus that makes it behave like a magnet.

Hounsfield believed that NMR signals emitted by cancerous cells are different from those emitted by healthy cells.

Raw Materials

The primary functioning parts of an MRI scanner include an external magnet, gradient coils, RF (radio frequency) equipment, and a computer. Other components include an RF shield, a power supply, NMR probe, display unit, and a refrigeration unit.

The external magnet, also called the imaging magnet, is the largest component of the MRI scanner. It is responsible for creating the powerful, steady magnetic field that penetrates throughout the body part in which a possible disorder is being identified.

Three types of magnets are currently used—the superconducting magnet, the resistive magnet, and the permanent magnet. Superconducting magnets, made of superconducting wire, are the most commonly used in MRI scanners. The superconducting wire is so called because it conducts, or transmits, electricity with no resistance at temperatures near absolute zero. The wire is made of a niobium-titanium alloy embedded in copper and is supercooled with liquid helium and liquid nitrogen. This type of magnet carries electricity without energy loss and, therefore, generates larger magnetic fields for higher-quality imaging.

A resistive magnet, as its name implies, creates a magnetic field by resistance to electric current in aluminum wire that is wrapped around an iron core. The magnet requires a great amount of electricity. It also requires water cooling since the resistance generates heat.

The third type of magnet used is a permanent magnet. It is made of ferromagnetic material, which generally contains iron, nickel, or cobalt. It is quite large and heavy and does not require electricity to run. Although the magnetic field in this magnet is always present, the stability of the magnetic field is not reliable.

The three gradient coils used in the MRI scanner are also magnets. These resistive magnets are positioned inside the main magnet and are kept at room temperature. While the main magnet subjects the patient to

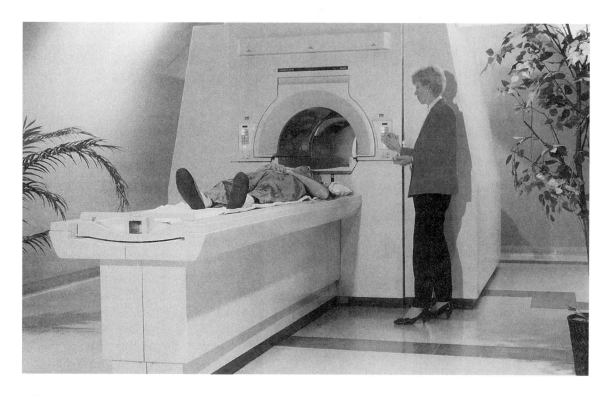

MRI scans are painless, requiring the patient to lie still while the machine scans a part of the body. *Reproduced by permission of Custom Medical Stock Photo.*

an intense, steady magnetic field, the gradient magnets provide varying strengths of magnetic fields to produce gradients, or variations, in the main magnetic field. The gradient coils help obtain the three-dimensional information needed for accurate images.

The RF system plays many roles in an MRI scanner. First, it transmits the RF radiation that causes the atoms in the tissue to emit a signal. Next, it receives the emitted signal and makes it louder so that a computer can use the information to construct an image on a television screen. RF coils are the primary pieces of hardware in the RF system. Different coils are available for the different body parts. The coil is usually positioned along the body part that is being scanned. Several types of RF coils are used. In newer models of MRI scanners, an RF shield is part of the machine. The shield is an aluminum sheet that reduces RF interferences.

The computer controls all parts of the MRI scanner. It controls the RF signals sent and stores the signals received. The computer processes all the information and then forms images of the body part being scanned.

resistive magnet: A magnet that creates a magnetic field by the resistance to electric current in aluminum wire that is wrapped around an iron core. It requires a great amount of electricity and water cooling.

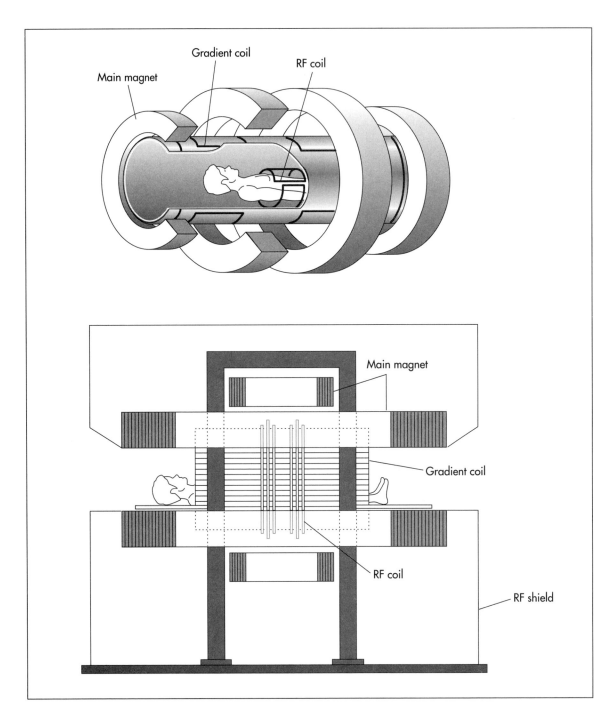

The components of a magnetic resonance imaging scanner. The patient is placed on a table that slides inside the machine.

The Manufacturing Process

The individual parts of an MRI scanner are typically manufactured separately and then assembled into a large unit. These units are extremely heavy, sometimes weighing over 100 tons (102 metric tons).

Magnet

1 The superconducting magnet is the type of magnet most commonly used in an MRI scanner. The basic design consists of coils of conductive (capable of transmitting electricity) wire, a cooling system, and a power supply. The coils are made by wrapping wire around a cylindrical tube through which electric current is passed. The wire is made from threads of a niobium-titanium alloy embedded in copper. To create the necessary magnetic field, several coils are used.

2 The coils are immersed in a vessel of liquid helium. This lowers their temperature to where they would not resist the flow of electricity, which can cause loss of energy. To help maintain a stable low temperature, the vessel is surrounded by two more vessels containing other coolants, such as liquid nitrogen. This whole assembly is then suspended with thin rods in a vacuum-sealed container. A power source is hooked up to the magnetic coils. The power source is used only when the magnets need to be energized. The cylindrical magnet is attached to a patient support, which is a movable table that brings the patient into the magnetic field.

Gradient coils

3 The three gradient coils are resistive magnets, each of which is made by winding thin strips of copper or aluminum in a specific pattern. The coils are strengthened by adding epoxy into their structure. The width of the coil is designed so that it is large enough to prevent claustrophobia (fear of being in an enclosed space) in the patient, but not so large that it requires significant energy to operate. The gradient coils are typically shielded to prevent interfering eddy currents (electrical current set by alternating magnetic fields).

RF System

4 The electrical components of the RF system may be produced by an outside manufacturer and then assembled by the MRI manufacturer. These components are attached to the RF transmitter and receiv-

superconducting magnet: A magnet whose magnetic field is produced by electric current in wires made of a superconducting material, such as niobium-titanium. Such material transmits electricity with no resistance at temperatures near absolute zero.

er coils. The coils are made of conducting copper that can create a vibrating magnetic field.

5 Different types of RF coils are designed for different parts of the body. A surface coil has a simple design, consisting of a loop of wire that may be circular or rectangular. It is used for imaging the shoulder or the spine and is placed directly on the patient. A bird cage coil, which is placed inside the gradient coils, is used for imaging the head and brain, while a paired saddle coil is used for the knees. A single turn solenoid coil is used for imaging the extremities, such as the wrists. Each type of coil is attached to a power source.

Computer

6 The computer, which is supplied by a computer manufacturer, is modified and programmed for the MRI scanner. Attached to the computer are the user interface, the Fourier transformer, the signal converter, and a preamplifier. A display device and a laser printer also come with the computer.

Final Assembly

7 Each MRI component is assembled together and placed into an appropriate frame. The whole scanner is put together at the hospital or other medical facility where it will be used. The magnet is typically transported in an air-suspended vehicle for a smoother ride.

Quality Control

Throughout the manufacturing process, visual and electrical inspections of the MRI scanner are performed. The finished scanner is then test-

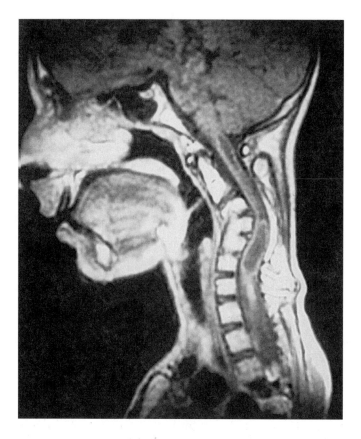

This magnetic resonance image, or MRI, shows the head and neck of a boy with spinal cancer. *Reproduced by permission of Photo Researchers, Inc.*

ed to make sure it is working properly. The testing is done under different environmental conditions, such as excessive heat and humidity. Most manufacturers establish their own quality specifications for their products. Various government agencies, such as the Department of Health and Human Services, and medical organizations have also proposed standards and performance recommendations.

The Future

MRI technology is young and has plenty of room for development. New models are not only shorter but also lighter. Some companies are looking into smaller-sized machines just for certain body parts, such as the foot or the hand. Open MRI scanners have solved the problem of patients who experience claustrophobia when placed in the conventional narrow tube. A vertically open MRI machine called the Magnetic Resonance Therapy comes with a tracker that can be attached to a patient's joint. The physician, who can stand on either side of the patient, can see, within seconds, what happens to the problem joint as the patient moves.

Dr. Raymond Damadian, the inventor of the MRI scanner and founder of FONAR, the first MRI manufacturing company, has several machines under development. These include a standup model, a breast scanner, and a room scanner with enough space for a team of surgeons and other equipment.

Researchers are addressing other factors that contribute to patient discomfort, such as the loud noises accompanying the scanning process. Toshiba Corporation of Japan has developed a noise-reduction technology in which the gradient coils, the source of the noise, are placed within a sealed vacuum chamber.

An area of interest in MRI application involves brain functional imaging. This is imaging that relates body function or thought to specific locations in the brain. When an area of the brain is active, blood flow to that area increases. MRI scanning, when done at a rapid speed, can see blood moving through the organs. Researchers believe MRI's future role in functional imaging may include helping evaluate the appropriateness and effectiveness of certain treatments for diseases, such as Alzheimer's and Parkinson's diseases.

WHAT'S ALL THAT RACKET?

Most MRI scanners make a loud, hammering noise during the imaging process. When electricity passes through the gradient coil, which is inside the main magnet, a force acts on the passing electric current. This force switches the electrical current on and off, causing vibration, which in turn causes the gradient coil to produce a high-level noise. Patients are usually given earplugs or stereo headphones to muffle the noise.

For More Information

Books

Commission on Physical Sciences, Mathematics, and Applications. "Magnetic Resonance Imaging." In *Mathematics and Physics of Emerging Biomedical Imaging.* Washington, D.C.: National Academy Press, 1996.

Yount, Lisa. "The Better to See You." In *Medical Technology.* New York, NY: Facts On File, Inc., 1998.

Periodicals

"Raymond V. Damadian: Scanning the Horizon." *Scientific American* (June 1997): pp. 32–33.

Web Sites

Dalton, Louisa. "Two Magnets are Cheaper Than One: Stanford Engineers Construct an Inexpensive MRI Scanner." *Stanford University.* http://www.stanford.edu/dept/news/pr/01/mri321.html (accessed on July 22, 2002).

Gould, Todd A. "How Magnetic Resonance Imaging (MRI) Works." *How Stuff Works.* http://www.howstuffworks.com/mri.htm (accessed on July 22, 2002).

Hornak, Joseph P. "Imaging Hardware." *The Basics of MRI.* http://www.cis.rit.edu/htbooks/mri/chap-9/chap-9.htm (accessed on July 22, 2002).

Mascara

M ascara is a cosmetic (a beauty product) applied to the eyelashes to make them look thicker, longer, and darker. Mascaras have been used since ancient times. As far back as 4000 B.C.E., both Egyptian men and women used makeup to outline and decorate their eyes. The Egyptians used soot or mixed eye powder with animal fat to make eye cosmetics. The powders were usually made from green malachite (copper ore) or dark gray galena (lead ore). The present-day name for galena is kohl.

The Babylonians and ancient Greeks also used eye cosmetics, as did the Romans in later centuries. After the fall of the Roman Empire (476 C.E.), the use of cosmetics declined, although eye cosmetics continued to be used in Middle Eastern countries. During the Renaissance (fourteenth through sixteenth centuries), cosmetics were again used in Europe.

Modern Mascara

Before the 1900s, American women did not commonly wear cosmetics. Cosmetics were generally associated with prostitutes or other "sinful" women who painted their faces. However, as women fought for the right to vote and other opportunities that men enjoyed, such as to become lawyers and doctors, they started wearing makeup to assert their independence. In 1913, a chemist, T.L. Williams, created the first mascara out of Vaseline® petroleum jelly and coal dust, subsequently establishing the company Maybelline,

The color additive kohl is not approved for use in the United States. Kohl contains salts of lead or antimony and has been linked to poisoning in some people.

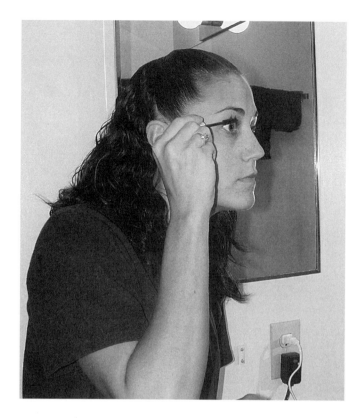

Mascara, which can be bought in a variety of colors, is applied to add emphasis to eye lashes, giving them a longer and darker look. *Photograph by Kelly A. Quin. Copyright © Kelly A. Quin. Reproduced by permission of the photographer.*

named after his sister Mabel and the ingredient Vaseline®. In 1917, Maybelline produced the first modern mascara, a cake mascara, which was applied to the eyelashes with a dampened brush. Helena Rubinstein (1871–1965) developed the first waterproof mascara in 1939. In the early 1960s, Maybelline produced the Ultra Lash Mascara, the first automatic mascara. Instead of a cake, the mascara came in a tube along with a grooved brush. When pulled from the tube, the brush was already coated with the mascara for easy application.

Raw Materials

There are many different formulas for making mascara. All contain pigments (coloring substances). The United States prohibits the use of pigments derived from coal or tar in eye cosmetics. Therefore, manufacturers have to use natural colors and artificial pigments. Most mascara formulas use carbon black for the black pigment and iron oxide for brown colors. Some recipes use the ultramarine blue color.

One common type of mascara consists of an emulsion of oils, waxes, and water. Oils may be mineral oil, lanolin, linseed oil, castor oil, oil of turpentine, eucalyptus oil, or sesame oil. The waxes used include beeswax, carnauba wax, or paraffin. Some formulas use alcohol. Lotion-based formulas contain stearic acid and stiffeners, such as ceresin and gum. The gum used may be gum tragacanth or methyl cellulose. Some mascaras have fine rayon fibers, which make the product more viscous (thick and sticky).

cake mascara: A mascara that comes in the form of a dry pressed cake and is applied to the eyelashes with a wetted brush.

cosmetic: A preparation that is applied to the face to make it more attractive.

The Manufacturing Process

There are two main types of mascara manufactured. One type is made using the anhydrous (without water) method. Mascaras that have a lotion base are made using the emulsion method.

Anhydrous method

1 The ingredients are carefully measured and weighed. They are then put into a mixing tank or kettle to make a small batch of 10 to 30 gallons (38 to 114 liters) of mascara. Heat is applied to melt the waxes, and the mixture is stirred using a propeller blade. The stirring continues until the mixture reaches a semi-solid state.

Emulsion method

2 Water and thickeners are combined to make a lotion or cream base. In a separate container, waxes and emulsifiers are heated, and pigments are added. The lotion base and wax-emulsifier mixture are combined in a homogenizer, or mixer. Unlike the tank used in the anhydrous method, the homogenizer has a closed lid that keeps out the air and prevents evaporation. The homogenizer blends the ingredients at a very high speed, breaking down the oils and waxes and holding them in suspension in the water. The homogenizer may contain as little as 5 gallons (19 liters) or as much as 100 gallons (380 liters) of mascara. The blending continues until the mixture reaches room temperature.

Filling

3 This step is used for both methods of manufacture. After the mascara solution has reached a semi-solid state (anhydrous method) or a cooled state (emulsion method), it is transferred to a tote bin. The tote bin is rolled to a filling area, and the mascara is poured into the hopper (a receptacle that holds the mascara) of a filling machine.

4 The filling machine pumps a measured amount (about 0.175 ounce, or 5 grams) of the mascara into glass or plastic bottles. The bottles are usually capped by hand. Samples are removed for inspection, and the rest are packaged for distribution.

Quality Control

Factory inspectors check for quality and purity at various stages of the manufacturing process. The ingredients are checked in the tank before mixing begins to ensure that the correct ingredients and proper amounts are in place. After the batch is blended, it is checked again. After bottling of the

---

EYELASH DYEING

Some beauty salons offer "permanent" eyelash and eyebrow dyeing by using hair dyes for coloring. According to the U.S. Food and Drug Administration (FDA), no natural or artificial color additives have been approved for such use at home or at beauty salons. When misused on eyelashes or eyebrows, hair dyes could cause serious reactions, including blindness or even death.

---

emulsion: A suspension of small beads of one liquid within another liquid with which the first liquid will not mix; for example, oil in water.

kohl: A cosmetic used by women, especially in Asia and the Middle East, as an eye makeup. It usually consists of salts of metals, such as lead and antimony.

pigment: A coloring substance.

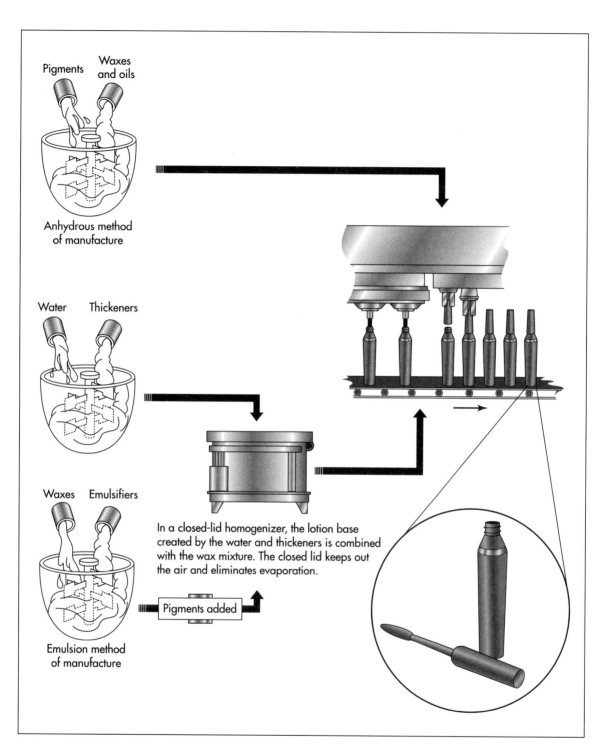

Mascara can be manufactured using the anhydrous method or the emulsion method.

mascara batch is completed, samples representing the beginning, middle, and end of the batch are taken. These samples are tested for chemical composition, as well as for impurities from microorganisms.

Interestingly, the federal government does not require mascara manufacturers to seek approval or review of their products before selling them to the public. Manufacturers may use any ingredient, except for color additives and a number of prohibited ingredients. The U.S. Food and Drug Administration (FDA) can regulate these products only after they are already in the market. If a certain product proves dangerous after consumers have used them, the FDA has to go through the Justice Department in order to take action, including inspecting the cosmetic factory and collecting mascara samples.

The Future

Cosmetic companies do not seem to run out of creative ideas when it comes to mascara. Today, mascaras not only darken, lengthen, and thicken, they also curl, soften, and condition lashes. Some boast of having ingredients that fight bacteria that may invade the eyes. Ingredients found in hair products, such as vitamin E, panthenol, and ceramide, are being added to mascara formulas. Aside from the standard colors of black and brown, other colors are available, such as burgundy, blue, green, and violet. This assortment of colors and pearlized mascaras are popular with young women. Some companies have even come out with mascaras that thicken the lashes to give the impression of false lashes.

For More Information

Periodicals

Kunzig, Robert. "Style of the Nile: Re-creating the Chemistry and Cosmetics of Queen Nefertiti." *Discover.* (September 1999): pp. 80–83.

Lewis, Carol. "Clearing Up Cosmetic Confusion." *FDA Consumer.* (May–June 1998): pp. 6–11.

Web Sites

"Eye Products." *U.S. Food and Drug Administration.* http://www.cfsan.fda.gov/~dms/cos-821.html (accessed on July 22, 2002).

suspension: A mixture of very fine particles of solid in a liquid, but in which the solids are not dissolved in the liquid.

waterproof: Resistant to water penetration.

Illes, Judith. "Ancient Egyptian Eye Makeup." *Tour Egypt Monthly.* http://www.egyptmonth.com/mag09012000/mag4.htm (accessed on July 22, 2002).

"On the Teen Scene: Cosmetics and Reality." *U.S. Food and Drug Administration.* http://www.cfsan.fda.gov/~dms/cos-813.html (accessed on July 22, 2002).

Microwave Oven

Reproduced by permission of Fieldmark Publications.

A microwave oven is an appliance that cooks or warms up food using microwaves produced by an electronic vacuum tube called a magnetron. The magnetron converts electricity to electromagnetic radiation (the microwaves), which is made up of waves of electric and magnetic energy. Once generated by the magnetron, the microwaves travel through a metal enclosure called a waveguide to a stirrer fan, which distributes the microwaves into the cooking cavity. Inside the cooking area, the microwaves are absorbed by the food, which is cooked or heated in a few minutes or seconds.

About 95 percent of American households own a microwave oven.

Efficient cooking with microwaves

Microwaves can be used in cooking because of certain characteristics. They pass through many types of glass, plastic, ceramic, and paper. They are reflected by metal, and they are absorbed by food. In microwave cooking, the microwaves act on the water molecules in the food, causing them to vibrate. The vibration causes friction, which generates heat, thereby cooking the food. Microwaves cook food more efficiently than conventional ovens because they act only on the food, unlike regular ovens which heat the oven walls and the air around the food. And since microwaves change to heat once they are absorbed by the food, the food does not get contaminated with the electromagnetic radiation.

First microwaved foods

The ability of microwave energy to cook food was discovered in 1945 by an engineer in the Raytheon Company. Percy L. Spencer (1894–1979) was inspecting a magnetron at work. (During World War II [1939–45], the magnetron tube had been used in radar systems.) Spencer discovered that a chocolate bar in his pocket had melted even though he had not felt any heat from the magnetron. Next, Spencer exposed some popcorn kernels to the magnetron, and, sure enough, the kernels popped.

Spencer discovered that, when confined to a metal enclosure, microwaves produced by the magnetron tube excite certain molecules, such as water found in food, causing the food to increase in temperature and eventually get cooked. The first microwave oven, called Radarange, developed by Spencer and the Raytheon Company, was about the size of a refrigerator. It was used in commercial food preparations, and cost about $3,000. In 1955, slightly smaller versions were sold as home appliances, but they were still expensive, and people were not sure they wanted an appliance that they thought emitted "radar waves."

Fast food, fast bucks

In 1967, Amana, a Raytheon division, introduced the first countertop models at a cost of $495. By the mid-1970s, microwave ovens were outselling gas ranges. Fears about the potential dangers of microwaves had dissipated, and different companies were manufacturing microwave ovens for home use. Since then, microwave ovens have become a popular kitchen fixture. About 95 percent of American households own a microwave oven. Related industries, such as microwavable foods and utensils designed to be used especially for microwave cooking, have also grown rapidly.

Design

A microwave oven has a front panel that allows the user to program the oven. The panel shows the cooking time, the power level, the time of day, and other information. The door has a window with a perforated (having small holes) metal shield that enables the user to view the food

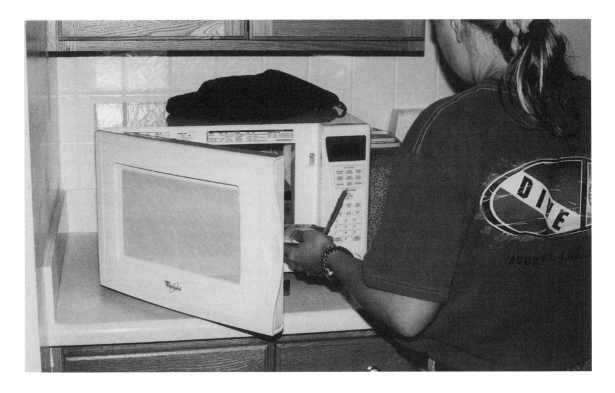

Popcorn is a favorite, easy-to-make snack for microwave owners. *Photograph by Kelly A. Quin. Copyright © Kelly A. Quin. Reproduced by permission of the photographer.*

while it is cooking. Microwaves cannot go through the holes to cause any harm because the holes are smaller than the wavelengths of the microwaves. As a result, microwaves simply bounce off the shield to act on the food. An oven light is also included.

The various electronic motors, relays, and control circuits (the routes through which electricity flows) are situated on the outer casing, to which the oven cavity is bolted, or fastened. The cooking cavity may contain a round, glass turntable on which the food dish is placed. The turntable rotates the food dish for even cooking. Instead of a turntable, the cooking cavity may just have a stationary (nonmoving) glass dish, which fits the bottom of the cavity.

Near the top of the cooking cavity is the magnetron tube, which produces the microwaves. The microwaves are funneled through a metal tube called a waveguide and into a stirrer fan. The fan distributes the microwaves evenly within the oven. Manufacturers use different methods to circulate the microwaves to achieve even cooking. Some use dual stirrer

interlocking switch: A safety switch that prevents the production of microwaves when the microwave oven door is open.

fans located on opposite walls. Others, in addition to the stirrer fan on top of the cavity, use entry ports (openings) at the bottom of the cavity so that microwaves enter through both the top and bottom.

Raw Materials

The outer covering of a microwave oven is usually a one-piece sheet metal enclosure. The door and the panels of the cooking cavity are made of stainless steel or galvanized steel (steel that has been coated with a thin layer of zinc to protect against rusting). A coating of acrylic enamel is also applied to the panels. The cooking surface is generally made of ceramic or glass. The cooking cavity is usually painted with a light color so that it is easy to see from outside the oven.

Between the cooking cavity and the oven walls, electromechanical components and controls consist of timer motors, switches, and relays. Also inside these walls are the magnetron tube, the waveguide, and the stirrer fan, all made of metal. The hardware that links the different components are made up of metal and plastic parts, including gears, pulleys, belts, nuts, screws, washers, and cables.

The Manufacturing Process

Most parts of the modern microwave oven are mounted in the area behind the front panel, between the sidewall of the cooking cavity and the chassis sidewall. Manufacturers aim to make ovens that are not too bulky. Therefore, they make sure the parts are efficiently situated within the available space, allowing enough room for the great amount of heat generated by the magnetron.

magnetron: A vacuum tube in which electrons traveling from the cathode (negative pole) to the anode (positive pole) are controlled by electric and magnetic fields to produce microwaves.

The cooking cavity and door

1 The manufacture of a microwave oven starts with the cooking cavity and the door. The cavity panels are formed using automatic metal-forming presses that can make twelve to fifteen parts per minute. In metal-forming, pressure is applied by the press on metal, changing its shape to form the cavity parts. The panels are rinsed in alkaline cleaner to

remove dirt or oil. Then, they are rinsed with water to remove the alkaline solution.

2 The cavity panels and door are treated with zinc phosphate to prepare them for electro-deposition, during which the pieces are immersed in a paint tank and electric current is used to apply the paint. Then, the pieces are moved through a paint-bake operation to set the paint coating at 300 degrees Fahrenheit (149 degrees Celsius) for twenty minutes.

3 After the door is painted, a perforated metal shield is attached to the window opening. The shield reflects microwaves but allows light to enter the cavity. The door will not be attached to the cavity until after the chassis, or main framework, is assembled.

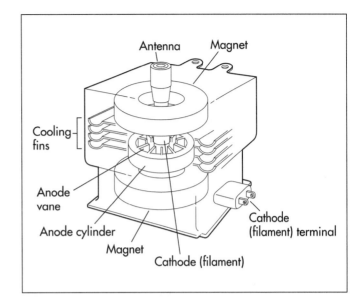

The magnetron tube generates the microwaves in a microwave oven. Metal cooling fins help get rid of the heat produced by the magnetron.

The magnetron tube subassembly

4 The magnetron tube consists of a filament heater, a metal anode, two magnets, and an antenna. The filament, which functions as the cathode, is enclosed in a ring-shaped metal anode. Then the cathode and the anode are sandwiched between two magnets. These components make up the assembly that will generate the microwaves. A metal strap holds the complete assembly together. Metal cooling fins, which are welded to the anode cylinder, help get rid of the heat produced by the magnetron. A thermal protector is mounted directly on the magnetron to prevent damage to the tube from overheating.

5 An antenna enclosed in a glass tube is connected to the anode cylinder. Then, the air within the magnetron tube is pumped out to create a vacuum. The antenna is connected to the waveguide, the hollow metal enclosure through which microwaves are transported from the magnetron tube to the cooking cavity. A blower motor is attached to the magnetron, and then a plastic fan is attached to the blower motor to provide cool air to the magnetron to prevent overheating.

stirrer: The fan that evenly distributes the microwaves into the cooking cavity.

waveguide: A metal enclosure on top of the cooking cavity through which microwaves produced by the magnetron travel to the cavity.

wavelength: The distance between the peaks of two successive waves of a microwave.

Chassis assembly

6 The chassis is the major framework onto which the various oven components will be attached. The chassis assembly work is done on a pallet, a work-holding device used with other tools. The chassis is placed on the pallet, and the cooking cavity is screwed on to the chassis. The door is attached to the cavity and chassis by means of hinges. The magnetron tube is then bolted to the side of the cavity and chassis.

7 The electric circuit of the oven consists of the transformer (which generates the high-voltage, or powerful electricity, required to operate the magnetron tube), an oil-based capacitor (which receives and stores electric current), and a rectifier (which changes the alternating current from the transformer into the direct current needed by the magnetron). All of these are mounted directly on the chassis, close to the magnetron tube.

Stirrer fan

8 The stirrer fan that circulates the microwaves is mounted on top of the cooking cavity. Some manufacturers use a pulley to operate the fan from the magnetron blower motor. Others use a separate stirrer motor attached directly to the fan. After the stirrer fan is attached, a stirrer shield is screwed on top of the fan assembly. The shield prevents dirt and grease from entering the waveguide, where they could produce sparks and damage the magnetron tube.

Control switches, relays, and motors

9 The cook switch provides power to the transformer by energizing a cook relay and a timer. The cook relay, also called a power relay, allows the control board to turn the microwave source off and on. The relay is mounted close to the power transformer, while the timer is mounted on the control board. Also mounted on the control board are a light switch for viewing the cooking cavity and a timer bell that rings when the cooking cycle is complete.

A number of interlocking switches, also called safety switches, are mounted near the top and bottom of the door area. These switches pre-

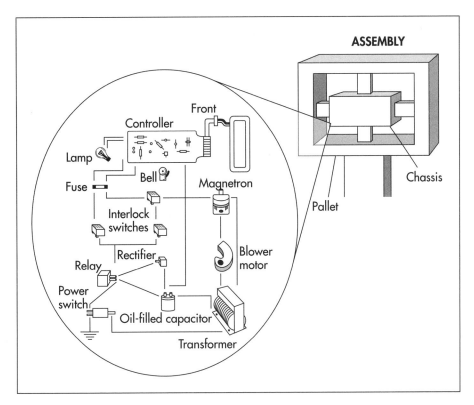

ASSEMBLY

Front

Controller

Lamp

Fuse

Bell

Magnetron

Interlock switches

Rectifier

Relay

Power switch

Oil-filled capacitor

Transformer

Blower motor

Pallet

Chassis

The chassis or frame is mounted in a pallet for the main assembly operation.

vent the production of microwaves when the door accidentally opens during cooking.

Front panel

10 Also attached to the chassis is the front panel, which allows the user to select the various settings and features available for cooking. Mounted behind the front panel is the control board, which is an electronic board that controls the various programmed operations when the switches are pushed on the front panel. This board is connected to the front panel and other components by means of plug-in sockets and cables.

Making and assembling the case

11 The outer case of the microwave oven is made from sheet metal, made by pressing steel between rollers. The sheet metal is formed into a wraparound case and fitted with a bottom

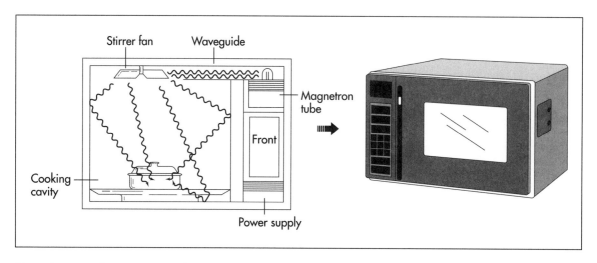

The antenna on the magnetron tube connects to the wave guide, which transports the microwaves to the stirrer fan. The fan points the microwaves into the cooking cavity where they heat the food inside.

plate, also made of steel. The finished case is slipped onto the preassembled oven and bolted to the main chassis. Finally, power cords and dial knobs, if any, are attached to the oven.

Testing and packaging the oven

12 Most manufacturers run the oven from fifty to one hundred hours continuously as part of the testing process. After testing is complete, a robot palletizer records the model and serial data of the oven for inventory purposes. A robot palletizer, which is fitted with a gripper unit, is also used in many industries for loading finished products onto pallets, or platforms. Finally, the microwave oven is sent to the packaging area.

Quality Control

Strict quality control throughout the manufacturing process is very important. Radiation that is emitted by the microwave oven can burn anyone exposed at high levels for prolonged periods. A computer-controlled scanner is used to measure radiation leaks around the door, window, and back of the oven. Other scanners check antenna radiation, as well as the seating of the magnetron tube. Each scanner operation passes on information to the next operation so that problems can be corrected.

The Code of Federal Regulations, revised as of April 1, 2001, limits the amount of radiation that can leak from a microwave oven to "1 milliwatt per

There are several different brands of microwaves available at stores, each with different colors, styles, and features. *Photograph by Kelly A. Quin. Copyright © Kelly A. Quin. Reproduced by permission of the photographer.*

square centimeter at any point 5 centimeters or more from the external surface of the oven, measured prior to acquisition by a purchaser, and, thereafter, 5 milliwatts per square centimeter at any such point." The regulation also requires all ovens to have a minimum of two safety interlocks to prevent the production of microwaves if the door accidentally opens during cooking.

The Future

Manufacturers continue to develop various models and new applications to appeal to new users and repeat consumers. Like other industries that are taking advantage of the popularity of the Internet, the microwave industry has introduced the so-called Internet microwave oven. The oven can be connected to the Internet to access recipes and other cooking information for automatic food preparation. Several companies plan to market their products in the near future.

Other new developments include a microwave oven with special brackets that allow installation anywhere in the kitchen, including inside wall cabinets and over islands (the freestanding areas usually found in the middle of the kitchen). Some models have the control panel located behind the oven door, thus giving the oven an overall sleek appearance. A trendy model that appeals to many of today's consumers is patterned after a popular computer monitor that comes in colors of red, orange, green, and blue.

In 2000 two Massachusetts inventors received a patent for a microwave oven that can be installed in a car's glove compartment. The oven would be powered by the car's battery and the controls would be mounted on the dashboard. The oven comes with a bin that could store things when the oven is not being used. The oven would only work when the bin is not in place.

For More Information

Books

Davidson, Homer L. *Troubleshooting and Repairing Microwave Ovens.* 4th ed. New York, NY: The McGraw-Hill Companies, Inc., 1997.

Microwave Oven Radiation. Washington, D.C.: Center for Devices and Radiological Health, U.S. Department of Health and Human Services, 2000.

Periodicals

"Short-Order Cooks: Very Good Microwave Ovens Are Cheaper Than Ever." *Consumer Reports* (January 2002): pp. 48–51.

Web Sites

Bloomfield, Louis A. "Microwave Ovens." *How Things Work.* http://howthings work.virginia.edu/microwave_ ovens.html (accessed on July 22, 2002).

"Explosive Cooking." *Discover.* http://www.discover. com/oct_issue/break cooking.html (accessed on July 22, 2002).

"Microwave Cooking for Today's Families." *U.S. Department of Agriculture.* http://www.foodsafety.gov/~fsg/fs-mwave.html (accessed on July 22, 2002).

"Microwave Ovens." *University of Colorado.* http://www.colorado.edu/physics/2000/microwaves (accessed on July 22, 2002).

Mosquito Repellent

Photograph by Edward S. Ross. Reproduced by permission of photographer.

A mosquito repellent is a substance designed to keep away mosquitoes, thereby preventing them from biting humans and feeding on human blood. It typically contains an active ingredient that repels mosquitoes and secondary ingredients that, among other things, dilute the active ingredient to a desired concentration and help in releasing the active ingredient when needed. Mosquito repellents are available as creams, lotions, oils, and sticks, which are applied directly on the skin. They also come as aerosol and pump-spray products, which are used on the skin and to treat clothing. Mosquito repellents are different from insecticides in that the latter are used to kill insects.

More than one-third of the U.S. population uses a DEET-based insect repellent each year.

Do they really work?

Various substances have been used to repel mosquitoes. These include smoke, tar, mud, and oils derived from plants, such as citronella, cedar, geranium, and peppermint.

Citronella oil, derived from the Southeast Asian grass citronella, was the first truly effective mosquito repellent. Citronella had been used for centuries for medicinal purposes. In 1901, it was discovered that citronel-

Swamps and rivers are the perfect breeding grounds for mosquitoes. *Reproduced by permission of the Louisiana Office of Tourism.*

la used as a hairdressing fragrance could repel mosquitoes. However, the oil evaporates quickly and, therefore, lasts only a short time. Citronella oil is also used as the active ingredient in candles or coils that are burned outdoors to produce smoke that repels mosquitoes. They have been found effective only if air movement is minimal.

Manufacturers of tablets containing garlic, brewer's yeast, or Vitamin B1 claim that their products repel mosquitoes. Some electronic devices that vibrate or emit high-frequency sounds also make such claims. Scientists have found that some lotions advertised as insect repellents do not contain any repellent. Instead, the mineral oil in these lotions serves as a film that prevent insects from penetrating the skin.

aerosol: A substance packaged under pressure and released as a spray.

DEET: The active ingredient in the most widely used insect repellents.

emollient: A substance that softens the skin.

A government invention

During World War II (1939–45), American soldiers stationed in the Pacific carried insecticides in aerosol cans to protect themselves against mosquitoes and other insects that carry diseases, such as malaria. After the war, in 1946, the U.S. Army and the U.S. Department of Agriculture jointly developed the repellent ingredient DEET (N,N-diethyl-3-methylbenzamide, formerly known as N,N-diethyl-3-m-toluamide). DEET became available to the public in 1957. Since then, thousands of chemical products have been tested, but DEET remains the only active ingredient that delivers the effectiveness required of a useful mosquito repellent.

Repelling action

Mosquito repellents work by interfering with the insect's homing system. This homing system, located in the antennae, consists of chemical receptors. The chemical receptors are stimulated by lactic acid that naturally evaporates from the skin of warm-blooded animals. When a repellent ingredient, such as DEET, is applied to the skin, it evaporates, forming a barrier around the skin. The mosquito, therefore, is unable to "find" the person to bite.

Raw Materials

A mosquito repellent consists of active and inert, or inactive, ingredients. The active ingredient is mainly responsible for the product's usefulness, that is, it effectively discourages mosquito attacks on the treated human skin and/or clothing. The inert ingredients are not chemically active. They are added to the product to perform different functions. For example, fragrances make the product cosmetically acceptable.

DEET is the active ingredient in the most widely used insect repellents. According to the Environmental Protection Agency (EPA), more than one-third of the U.S. population uses a DEET-based insect repellent each year. More than two hundred million people worldwide use similar products.

Other repellent ingredients include the chemical substance dimethlyl-phthalate and plant-based repellents, such as citronella oil, lavender, lemongrass oil, and peppermint oil. It has been found that mixtures of different repellent ingredients are more effective than any one alone. The active ingredients in mosquito repellents generally make up about 5 to 30 percent of the final product.

patent: To obtain from the government the right to make and sell an invention for a certain period of time.

malaria: A serious disease spread by the bites of female mosquitoes. It is characterized by intense fever and may cause complications affecting the brain, blood, liver, and kidneys that can cause death.

The inert ingredients used in a mosquito repellent depend on the form that the product will take. Mosquito repellents are sold as aerosols, pumps, creams, lotions, oils, and sticks. Those that are sold as creams or lotions are essentially skin creams, with a certain level of DEET added. They mainly consist of water, emollients (skin softeners), fatty alcohol, fragrance, and surfactants (substances that keep the liquid ingredients spread out). They act both as a skin moisturizer and a repellent. However, they are not as effective as aerosols or pumps because the active ingredient cannot evaporate easily.

Aerosols, the most common form for mosquito repellents, consist of a solvent, a propellant, and other ingredients. The solvent, propyl alcohol or ethanol, dilutes the active ingredient to a specific concentration. It also keeps all the materials mixed so the product will remain effective even after long storage. The propellant is a high-pressure gas that forces the repellent out of the container when the button on top of the can is pushed down. Propellants used include liquefied hydrocarbon gases, such as propane, butane, or isobutene, hydrofluorocarbons, and dimethyl ether. Fragrances and emollients are added for cosmetic appeal, as are substances to prevent rust and keep the product stable (maintain its chemical and physical characteristics).

The aerosol can is typically made of tin-plate steel, or steel that has been coated with tin to prevent any interaction between the steel and the repellent ingredients. The valve is a device that will open or close to control the movement of the repellent within the can when the actuator button is pushed down. The valve has three sections—the long plastic tube called a dip tube that extends from the bottom of the can to the top, the valve body, and the actuator button. When the actuator button is pushed down, the propellant pushes the mosquito repellent up the dip tube and out through a small opening that runs through the button. The liquid repellent comes out as a fine spray.

The Manufacturing Process

Since most mosquito repellents are marketed in the form of aerosols, the following steps describe the production of repellents contained in aerosols. The manufacturing process consists of two steps—the production of a large batch of the repellent formula and its packaging into aerosol cans. Other forms of mosquito repellents, such as creams and lotions, are made in the same manner. However, the filling process is not as complex.

Compounding

1 The raw materials are mixed in the compounding area. For an aerosol, the alcohol is pumped into a large stainless steel tank. Then, the DEET, fragrance, and emollients are manually poured in and allowed to mix. At this stage of the production, all the other ingredients are added, except the propellant. Since some materials are flammable, special precaution is taken to prevent explosion, such as using spark-proof electrical outlets and blast-proof walls.

2 When the batch is made, a sample is tested to make sure the product meets specific standards. The repellent is then pumped to the filling lines to make the finished product.

Filling

3 The filling line consists of a series of machines connected by a conveyor belt system. The machines assemble all the components (parts) to make the finished mosquito repellents. The first machine has a large hopper, or bin, containing empty cans. The cans are set in an upright position and fed onto the conveyor belt.

4 The cans are moved along the conveyor belt and cleaned with a jet of compressed air to remove any impurities. As the cans pass through a filling carousel, they are filled with a predetermined amount of repellent.

5 The next machine has a hopper that contains valves, which are sorted and aligned. The filled cans are topped with valves. A valve crimping machine attaches the valves to the cans. Depending on the filling method, the propellant is either injected through the valves under high pressure or injected into the cans before the valves are permanently attached.

6 After the cans are capped, they are immersed in a tank filled with hot water. The immersed cans are checked for escaping bubbles that would indicate a propellant leak. The high temperature of the water also raises the pressure inside the can. The increased pressure would cause any weak spots in the can to fail to operate. This quality-control step weeds out damaged cans.

BLOOD SUCKERS

Only female mosquitoes bite, using a needle-like sucking tube called the proboscis, to fill herself with blood from warm-blooded mammals and birds. Mosquitoes use the protein in blood to produce over two hundred eggs per blood meal. A female mosquito needs a blood meal each time she produces eggs.

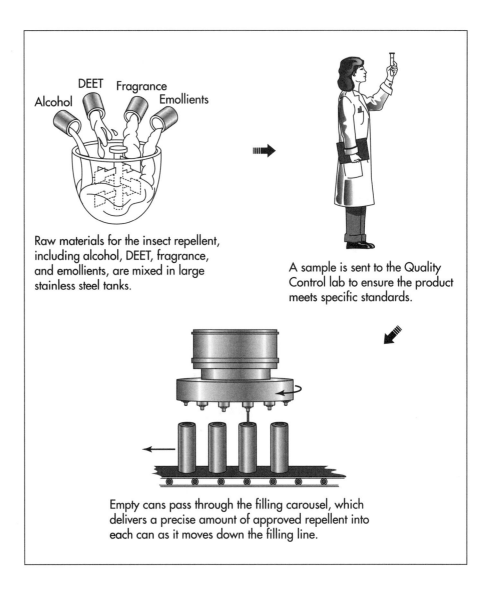

Raw materials for the insect repellent, including alcohol, DEET, fragrance, and emollients, are mixed in large stainless steel tanks.

A sample is sent to the Quality Control lab to ensure the product meets specific standards.

Empty cans pass through the filling carousel, which delivers a precise amount of approved repellent into each can as it moves down the filling line.

7 After the waterbath, the cans are dried by high-pressure air jets. Other parts, such as the depressible button and the overcap, are added. Then, a label or printing is added.

8 High-speed production lines like the one just described can manufacture about two hundred or more canned repellents per minute. The finished aerosol cans are moved to the packaging area, where they are boxed, typically a dozen cans to a box. Lastly the boxes are shipped to the distributors.

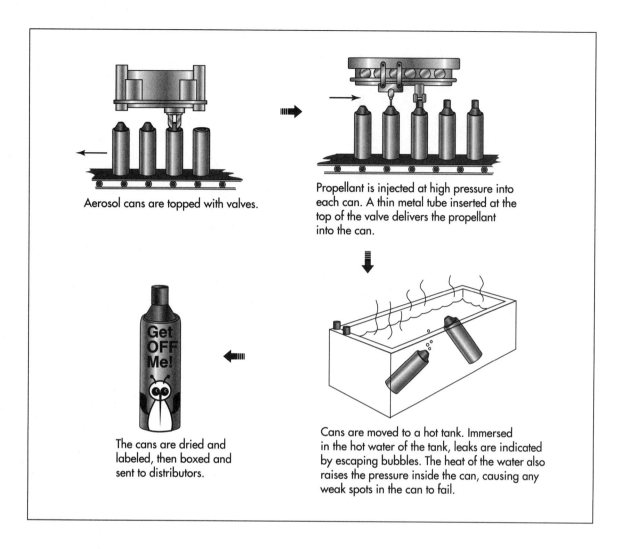

Aerosol cans are topped with valves.

Propellant is injected at high pressure into each can. A thin metal tube inserted at the top of the valve delivers the propellant into the can.

Cans are moved to a hot tank. Immersed in the hot water of the tank, leaks are indicated by escaping bubbles. The heat of the water also raises the pressure inside the can, causing any weak spots in the can to fail.

The cans are dried and labeled, then boxed and sent to distributors.

Quality Control

Tests are performed at various points of production. This is to ensure that the finished products are consistent throughout the manufacturing process, will remain effective over a long period of time, and are safe to use.

Before the start of production, the incoming raw materials are checked against set specifications. The empty cans are checked for dents, rust, and other weaknesses.

During the different points along the filling line, samples of the repellent are tested for such characteristics as the level of active ingredient, pressure, spray rate, and spray pattern. The finished cans are also checked

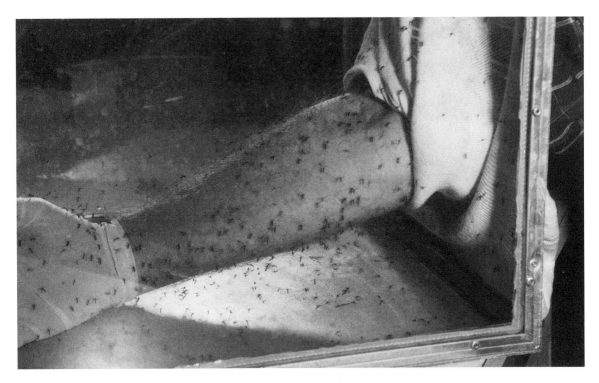

Researchers often test the effectiveness of different mosquito repellents by putting the product on their arm, which is then placed inside a mosquito-filled container. *Reproduced by permission of Corbis Corporation.*

to see if they are dispensing the repellent properly. Long-term studies may also be done to establish that the cans do not show undue signs of chemical changes, such as rust.

The Future

In the last twenty years, scientists at the Agricultural Research Service of the U.S. Department of Agriculture (USDA) have tested about 16,000 new repellents as possible DEET alternatives. A repellent called piperdine may be a possible candidate. However, until studies of synthetic repellents are completed, DEET remains the most effective in repelling mosquitoes.

Both the USDA and the EPA believe that, when used as directed, mosquito repellents are safe for children. However, reported misuse of DEET-based repellents, especially among children, has prompted the EPA to impose labeling restrictions on products marketed for infants and children. The EPA considers as mislabeling any claim that a product is "child safe" or "for children." This includes pictures specifically targeted for children. In addition, manufacturers may not incorporate ingredients with food fragrances that may cause children to ingest the product.

For More Information

Books

Spielman, Andrew, and Michael D'Antonio. *Mosquito: A Natural History of Our Most Persistent and Deadly Foe, 2001.* New York, NY: Hyperion.

Periodicals

Petersen, Jack. "Mosquito Repellent." *Wing Beats.* (Winter 2000): pp. 11, 13.

Rivera, Rachel. "Killer Mosquitoes: Mosquito Bites Can Be Deadly." *Science World.* (March 11, 1998): pp.14–15.

Wu, Corina. "Mosquito Magnets: Identifying Skin Chemicals That Attract Mosquitoes." *Science News.* (April 22, 2000): pp. 268–271.

Web Sites

Floore, Tom. "Mosquito Information." *The American Mosquito Control Association.* http://www.mosquito.org/mosquito.html (accessed on July 22, 2002).

Photograph

Photograph by Kelly A. Quin. Copyright © Kelly A. Quin. Reproduced by permission of the photographer.

A photograph is an image made by light on a photosensitive (sensitive to light) material and then reproduced permanently on paper (the print) by a subsequent exposure to light. Photography is possible because light that is reflected back from the subject reacts with the silver halide crystals (silver compounds) on the film to form an image of the subject.

The term "photography" comes from the Greek words photos *(light) and* graphia *(writing). Early photographers thought of photography as writing with light.*

Waiting to be invented

Although early scientists knew that light can change silver compounds into silver metal (one of the basic ingredients for making photographs), photography was not invented until the early nineteenth century. As early as 1500, the first crude camera called the *camera obscura* was used by artists as a tracing tool. The *camera obscura*, or dark chamber, was a dark room in which light that was reflected off an external object passed through a small hole in the room and was projected as an upside-down image on the opposite wall. The *camera obscura* was later converted to a portable closet and then to a small box. In 1685, German monk Johann Zahn (1641–1707) outfitted the *camera obscura* with lenses, constructing a model of today's camera. Even then, no one thought to combine the two ingredients to produce photographs.

In 1727, Johann Schulze (1684–1744), a German professor of anatomy, discovered that silver salts turned dark when exposed to sunlight. He made images on silver salts but could not keep the images permanent. In 1777, Swedish chemist Carl Scheele (1742–1786) found that an image resulting from silver salts that had been exposed to light could be made permanent by washing away the unexposed salt with ammonia. However, no one put these two discoveries to use. Around 1800, English botanist Thomas Wedgwood (1771–1805) came close to inventing photography. To record specimens he had collected outdoors, such as leaves, he put them against leather that had been coated with silver salts and then exposed them to sunlight. The areas surrounding the object turned dark, leaving an outline of the object. Although Wedgwood is considered the first photographer, he could not keep his "sun pictures" from eventually darkening. Unfortunately, he had not heard of Scheele's discovery.

First photographs

It took more than twenty years for the first modern photographs to finally be produced. The first known permanent photograph was made by Joseph Nicéphore Niépce (1765–1833) in 1826. The French chemist coated a pewter plate with bitumen of Judea, a substance used in printmaking. He then put the plate in a *camera obscura* that was set on an upstairs windowsill in his home and exposed the plate for eight hours. (See sidebar.)

During the 1830s, French inventor Louis Jacques Mandé Daguerre (1787–1851) experimented with several photographic processes, some done in collaboration with Niépce. After the latter died in 1833, Daguerre went on to invent what became known as *daguerreotype*. He coated a copper plate with silver and exposed it to iodine vapor to form silver iodide. He developed the image with mercury vapor, and then made it permanent using a table salt bath. Daguerre's invention needed camera exposures of thirty minutes. In 1839, the French government bought the rights to the daguerreotype and shared the new invention with the world.

At around the same time in England, William Henry Fox Talbot (1800–1877) was developing a paper negative called calotype, from which any number of positive prints could be made. The calotype was light-sensitized with silver chloride. Unlike daguerreotype, the calotype had an exposure time of about one minute or less. In 1844, Talbot produced the first book in the world illustrated with photographs, calling it *The Pencil of Nature*. To "fix" (make permanent) his photographs, Talbot used the discovery of another Englishman, John Herschel (1792–1871), an astronomer and a chemist. About twenty years earlier in 1819, Herschel had found that hyposulfate could be used as a fixing agent to dissolve the unexposed sil-

aperture: Opening of camera lens.

darkroom: A room in which photographic films and prints are processed, either in complete darkness or illuminated by a safelight that does not act on light-sensitive materials.

development: The process by which the latent image on the film is treated with chemicals to produce the negative from which the final paper print is made.

emulsion: A mixture of silver halide crystals in gelatin, used to coat photographic film.

exposure: The process of allowing light from a subject being photographed to reach the light-sensitive photographic film in order to form an image.

An example of a daguerreotype photograph. *Reproduced by permission of Henry Ford Museum & Greenfield Village.*

ver salts. Like Talbot, he had used light-sensitive paper to produce photographs. In fact, Herschel was responsible for coining the terms "negative" and "positive." Although German astronomer Johann von Maedler (1794–1874) first used the the term "photography," from the Greek words *photos* (light) and *graphia* (writing) in 1839, Herschel is usually credited with coining the term because he first used it at a public lecture.

Wet plate, dry plate

In early 1851, British sculptor Frederick Archer (1813–1857) introduced the collodion negative, also called the wet plate. A polished sheet of glass was coated with collodion, or nitrated cotton, that had been dissolved in a solution of ether and alcohol. The glass was then immersed in silver compounds. The plate had to be used while still wet, although exposure took just two to three seconds, and the resulting prints were rich in details. Since the wet-plate negative required immediate development, photographers took portable darkrooms with them. Interestingly, despite this troublesome method of taking pictures, photographers everywhere in the world used the collodion process for more than twenty years, recording places never seen before, as well as such important events as the American Civil War (1861–65).

The introduction of the dry plate in 1871 not only freed photographers from having to take their darkrooms on location but also from having to use a tripod for cameras because the exposure time was as short as one-twenty-fifth of a second. English physician Richard Maddox (1816–1902) started using gelatin to bind silver salts on sheets of glass. Once the plates dried, they could be used any time and did not require immediate processing. During processing, the gelatin expanded to let the developing and fixing chemicals act on the negative silver salts without dislodging

fixing: The process of removing from photographic film the undeveloped silver halide crystals, resulting in a negative or print that cannot be affected by the further action of light.

them from the film. Gelatin emulsion could also be used to coat print papers. In the past, negatives had to be the same size as the final print. With the new type of papers, the dry-plate negatives could be made smaller, and the desired print sizes were made using an enlarger with an artificial light source. Maddox's dry-plate photography is the ancestor of today's photography.

Photography made easy

American George Eastman (1854–1932) learned about Maddox's dry-plate process and experimented with his own gelatin emulsions. By 1881, he was mass-producing dry plates for amateur photographers. In 1885, Eastman introduced a roll film wound around a spool with enough film for taking several pictures. Eastman's Kodak portable box camera, introduced in 1888, made photography quite practical. The camera contained a roll film for one hundred pictures. After all the film was exposed, the user mailed the camera to Eastman's company, which developed the film, made prints, and returned the camera reloaded with a fresh roll of film. The following year Eastman improved on his film by putting his gelatin-silver halide crystal emulsion onto celluloid, a transparent mixture of plant fibers and plastic. Both film processing and camera equipment have improved since Eastman's inventions, but the basic principles of photography have remained the same.

Raw Materials

Film

Modern film is made by coating light-sensitive ingredients onto a transparent (see-through) material, such as acetate. Film manufacture is a complicated process because a typical roll of film may contain twenty or more different layers that make up a thickness of less than one-thousandth of an inch.

The first step in the process is to grow silver halide crystals, the light-sensitive ingredients mainly responsible for capturing an image exposed to

REVISING HISTORY: THE OLDEST PHOTOGRAPH

Joseph Nicéphore Niépce is credited with taking what is considered the world's first photograph. The 1826 photograph has been on display at the University of Texas in Austin since 1964. The fuzzy picture, which can be seen only from certain angles, shows part of a rooftop and a portion of Niépce's home in France. In the 1990s, the National Library of France acquired what is said to be a photograph, also done by Niépce, that predates that picture: An 1825 photograph of a boy leading a horse.

gelatin: Protein made from animal skins and bones and used to bind light-sensitive silver halide crystals to photographic film.

latent image: The invisible image produced by light on photographic film before it is processed.

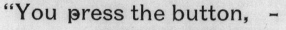

THE KODAK CAMERA.

"You press the button, -
- - - we do the rest."

The only camera that anybody can use without instructions. Send for the Primer, free.

The Kodak is for sale by all Photo stock dealers.

The Eastman Dry Plate and Film Co.,

Price $25.00—Loaded for 100 Pictures.   ROCHESTER, N. Y.

A full line Eastman's goods always in stock at LOEBER BROS,, 111 Nassau Street, New York.

This advertisement for Kodak's portable box camera appeared in the first issue of *The Photographic Herald and Amateur Sportsman* in November 1889. *Courtesy of Henry Ford Museum and Greenfield Village.*

negative: The developed photographic film in which the dark and light tones of the original image are reversed.

photosensitive: Sensitive to light.

silver halide: Compound of silver, such as silver bromide, silver chloride, and silver iodide, used for most photographic films.

light. These crystals are grown in solution from silver nitrate and halide ions (bromide, chloride, and iodide). After the crystals have reached the desired sizes and shapes, they are mixed in a gelatin base to form an emulsion.

In their original form, the silver halide crystals are sensitive only to blue light, and, therefore, need some improvements. The silver halide crystals and gelatin emulsion is melted and the crystals are coated with chemical agents to enhance their sensitivity to other colors. The melted emulsion is then applied on a transparent film.

The film may be coated with the emulsion of silver halide crystals and gelatin using different methods. One method involves dipping the film in a tray containing the melted emulsion. Excess liquid is removed by a knife edge or air jets. Another method involves passing the film under a funnel-shaped container called a hopper, which spreads the emulsion on the film. After coating, the emulsion is spread evenly on the film with rollers and transported to a cooling chamber where the emulsion assumes a semisolid state. The film is then sent through a heated chamber, which dries and hardens the emulsion.

The film can be coated with several layers of emulsion using these methods.

Certain coatings can also be added to control how the light is reflected on or absorbed by the film. For this purpose, dyes, carbon particles, or colloidal silver may be added. Finally, the film is painted with a gelatin overcoat to hold the inner layers in place and to seal the film. Generally, the thicker the layers of emulsion and the larger the size of the silver halide crystals, the more light-sensitive the film.

The final step involves winding the film onto spools, which are packaged in lightproof containers. When the consumer opens the container, he or she has to make sure the film is loaded into the camera immediately without exposing it to light.

Materials for film development and printing

In order to produce a negative from a photographic film, chemicals called developer solutions are used. The developer solutions consist of a reducing agent, a restrainer, and a preservative. The reducing agent (also called the developing agent) is designed to turn the silver halide crystals into metallic silver large enough to be seen by the naked eye. Some of the reducing agents used are hydroquinone and phenidone. The restrainer, such as potassium bromide, serves to protect the unexposed (not acted on by light) crystals from developing. The preservative is added to prevent premature reaction of the developing agent with oxygen in the air. Sodium sulfite is the preservative commonly used.

The paper used to print the final image from a negative is a high-quality paper made just for this purpose. Both sides of the paper have waterproof plastic layers. The face side is coated with light-sensitive silver halide crystals. As with the photographic film, gelatin is used to hold together the silver halide crystals and dyes in multiple layers. The paper is available in different grades, which vary in smoothness and shine.

Printing also requires an enlarger, or a projector, to increase the size of the image. Developing and toning solutions are also needed to control the intensity and color of the image. Other equipment needed for both developing and printing includes a developing tank, a developing spool (a cylinder for winding), trays, measuring glassware, thermometers, drying screens, timers, paper cutters, and mixing pails and stirring paddles.

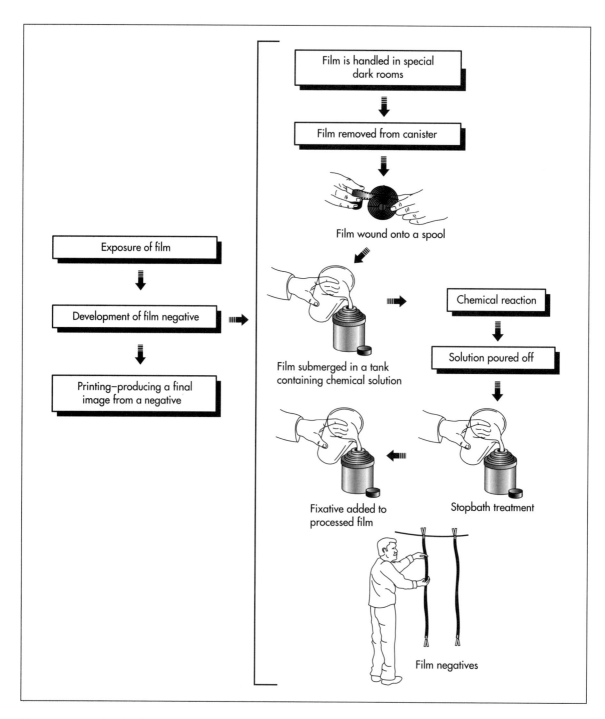

Three steps are involved in making a photograph—exposing the film to light (commonly referred to as taking a picture), developing the image, and making a printing of the image.

The Manufacturing Process

Three steps are involved in making a photograph—exposing the film to light (commonly referred to as taking a picture), developing the image, and making a printing of the image. The following steps discuss the general process of developing a 35-millimeter film into photographic prints.

Exposure

1 A film is ready for picture-taking once it is loaded inside the camera. When a camera takes a picture, the light reflected on the person or object passes through the lens, which focuses that light on the emulsion crystals of the film to reproduce the image of the person or object. The reaction between the emulsion and the light forms a latent (not yet seen) image on the film. The camera controls the light through a combination of the size of the aperture (opening in the lens) and the length of time the aperture stays open (the shutter speed). The photographer determines the appearance of the final photograph print by, among other things, varying these two factors.

Development

2 When all the film has been used, it can be developed. Development refers to the process by which the latent image on the film is treated with chemicals to produce the negative from which the final paper print will be made.

The film is developed in a darkroom illuminated with an orange light bulb called a safelight, which generally does not cause changes to the light-sensitive film. The film is removed from its canister and rolled onto a spool. For most films, this initial step has to be done in a completely dark room. The film is then submerged in a stainless steel or plastic developing tank and the tank lid is closed. Through a small hole in the tank, the developing chemicals are added. The gelatin in the film expands to allow the chemicals to penetrate the exposed areas of the film (the silver halide crystals changed by light during the picture-taking), while at the same time holding the crystals in place.

3 Next, the developing solution is poured off. The development process is stopped by the addition of dilute acetic acid, called the stop bath because it stops the film from overdeveloping. Then, the film is immersed in a fixing bath to make the image permanent. During fixing, the film is also made insensitive to light by dissolving any undeveloped silver halide crystals. Finally, the developed film is washed and rinsed to remove remaining chemicals. The film spool is then removed from the developing tank and hung to dry. The developed film is called a negative because it is the opposite of how it is seen by the eye. Those areas of the image that received the most light during exposure appear dark in the negative, while areas that received no light appear clear.

Printing

4 Printing is the process of producing a final image from a negative. The print made is usually bigger than the negative. The negative is placed in a machine called an enlarger, which uses a lens to focus light through the negative, projecting it onto a light-sensitive paper. In this manner, an enlarged image of the negative is formed on the silver halide crystals of the paper.

5 The print paper with the positive image (image that corresponds to the original subject taken) is then developed by a process similar to that used in developing the film. After the print is dry, it can be mounted on cardboard or other backing material. Reprints (additional prints of the same image) may be produced in a similar manner from the original negative or from a print.

Quality Control

The manufacture of photographic film is an exact process. The emulsion coatings of silver halides must be free of streaks and must be of uniform thickness to yield a quality film. Each stage of production is checked to ensure the finished product is free from defects. During development of both the negative and the print, areas of importance include the correct concentrations of chemicals in the development tank, as well as proper temperature and time of development. If the solutions are not the right concentration, the negative or the print may be overprocessed or underprocessed.

The Future

Although the fundamental principles of photography remain the same, advances continue to be made in the way pictures are taken. Some major developments include the Advanced Photo System (APS) camera and the digital camera. The APS technology is a cartridge-based alternative to 35-millimeter film. Unlike the 35-millimeter film that has to be threaded to a take-up spool in the camera, the APS cartridge has drop-in loading and unloading, which means that the photographer does not have to touch the film. Manufacturers claim this results in a higher proportion of well-developed films. In addition, the system allows photos of different formats from the same film cartridge, such as a standard print, a panoramic view, or a group picture. Recent designs include combining the APS technology with shoot-and-point capabilities using interchangeable zoom lenses.

The ease of sharing photographs instantly through computers has contributed to the increasing popularity of digital photography. Digital cameras do not use films. Instead, they use electronic sensors that convert light into digital code, or number code, which can be read by a computer. New models not only allow the manipulation of images to fit a postcard, but they also let the sender include text and voice messages.

In the meantime, chemists and other scientists employed by manufacturers of photographic films and papers continue to research technologies that would produce films and papers that not only yield better pictures but also pictures that last longer.

For More Information

Books

Bustard, Bruce I. *Picturing the Century: One Hundred Years of Photography from the National Archives.* Seattle, WA: University of Washington Press, 1999.

Langford, Michael. *Story of Photography.* 2nd ed. Oxford, England: Reed Educational and Professional Publishing Ltd., 1997.

Sills, Leslie. *In Real Life: Six Women Photographers.* New York, NY: Holiday House, 2000.

Web Sites

"History, Science, and Art of the Daguerreotype." *The Daguerreian Society.* http://www.daguerre.org (accessed on July 22, 2002).

Woodworth, Charles. "How Photographic Film Works." *Howstuffworks.* http://www.howstuffworks.com/film.htm (accessed on July 22, 2002).

FILM SPEED

Photographic films that have more layers of silver halide–gelatin emulsion and larger-sized silver halide crystals are generally more sensitive to light. The film's sensitivity to light is represented by the ISO (International Standards Organization) number (ASA, or American Standards Association, number for older cameras).The higher the ISO number, the more sensitive the film is to light, which means it has a higher film speed. For example, an ISO 400 film is a faster film than an ISO 200 film and, therefore, needs a shorter exposure to record an image. Hence, a 400-speed film might be a better choice when photographing fast-moving action, such as an athletic event, or a moving object.

Roller Coaster

Reproduced by permission of AP/Wide World Photos.

In the United States, approximately three hundred million people ride roller coasters every year.

A roller coaster is an amusement park ride made of a series of linked cars on a rail track supported by a wood or steel structure and shaped into rises, drops, twists, and turns. In the United States, approximately three hundred million people ride roller coasters every year.

In operation, the train of cars is pulled up a steep hill, called a lift hill, by a motorized linked chain. Anti-rollback mechanisms consisting of steel bars called anti-rollbacks (found on the track) and metal hooks called dogs (found under the cars) prevent a climbing train from rolling backward. If the train starts going backward, the anti-rollback dogs latch on to the steel bars to stop further movement. When the cars reach the top of the hill, they are released by the chain and are pulled downward by gravity through a series of drops, rises, and turns. Finally, the cars are slowed and then stopped at the starting point, where the passengers get out, and new passengers get on.

Thrill rides

The original roller coasters were ice slides in Russian fairs during the fifteenth and sixteenth centuries. The ride consisted of a steep incline of ice or a wooden slide covered with ice. Some rides had a few bumps for variation. A sand pile at the bottom of the slide stopped the sled from going any further.

Visitors from France are said to have borrowed the idea of the ride, calling it the Russian Mountains. Waxed wooden slides and wooden sleds with wheels were later built to afford year-round entertainment. By the early 1800s, the first roller coaster with a train of cars running on a track had become popular. As the popularity of the rides grew, operators built faster and more exciting coasters. However, the operators did not provide safety devices, and accidents frequently occurred. By the mid-1850s, people had lost interest in the rides, and they were closed down.

Mules on roller coasters

The American version of the first roller coaster started out as mine cars used to carry coal from the mountains down to barges in a canal below. In the early 1800s, the Mauch Chuck Switchback Railway in Pennsylvania used mules to haul empty mine cars up the mountain. The loaded cars and a separate car for the mules rode 18 miles (29 kilometers) downhill by gravity alone. Later on, steam engines replaced the mules.

When mining operations changed in 1874, the railroad began hauling sightseers instead of coal. A hotel and restaurant on the mountain added to the popularity of the one-dollar ride, which continued operation up to 1938 when the railroad closed.

Early roller coasters

In 1884, LaMarcus Thompson (1848–1919) built the Gravity Pleasure Switchback Railway ride in Coney Island, New York. This was the earliest true roller coaster, made of wood on a wooden support structure. Passengers climbed up the stairs and got on a car that faced sideways. The car was pushed down an incline, coasting over a series of gentle hills. For the return trip, the riders switched to another car, which was similarly operated. The nickel ride, which was made for sightseeing, traveled at a speed of six miles per hour.

In late 1884, Charles Alcoke built the second coaster in Coney Island. The Serpentine Railway was the first oval track and traveled at twelve miles per hour. The following year, Phillip Hinckle built the Gravity Pleasure Road, using a chain lift to haul the cars up the first hill, allowing the riders to board on the ground. The cars also faced forward.

By the 1920s, over 1,500 wooden roller coasters were operating in the United States. However, the economic hardships of the Great Depression (1929–1933) and the wartime material shortages during World War II (1939–1945) put an end to the roller coaster craze.

crosstie: A beam that is laid across the track to support the rails.

double dip: A drop that is interrupted by a short flattened section midway down the hill, thereby increasing the airtime, or feeling of weightlessness.

fiberglass: A lightweight, strong material made from compressed glass fibers.

g force: Stands for gravitational force, which is a measurement of the amount of gravity exerted on the passengers at different points of the roller coaster ride.

gravity: The force that pulls objects down toward the earth.

inversion: Part of the roller coaster track that turns riders upside down.

Roller coasters come in all different shapes and sizes, including this one in Wildwood, New Jersey, which takes its riders on an upside-down journey. *Reproduced by permission of Archive Photos.*

Modern roller coasters

It took more than two decades for roller coasters to make a comeback. In 1959, Walt Disney (1901–1966) opened the Matterhorn Bobsled ride at Disneyland in Anaheim, California. This was the first tubular steel coaster and consisted of cars that were constructed like bobsleds. However, it took the construction of John Allen's (1907–1979) new wooden coaster in 1972— Racer at Kings Island near Cincinnati, Ohio—to revive interest in roller coasters. Since then, higher and faster coasters have been constructed each year. As of early 2002, Superman: The Escape (Valencia, California), opened in 1997, was the fastest (100 miles per hour, or 161 kilometers) and tallest (415 feet, or 126 meters) roller coaster in the United States.

Raw Materials

The two types of roller coasters are wooden and steel coasters. Wooden coasters, sometimes called "woodies," use huge supporting structures consisting of horizontal beams supported by two pair of spreading legs at each end. These are called trestle-style structures. The wood, typically made of Douglas fir or southern yellow pine, is painted or treated to prevention deterioration. The wooden parts are supported on concrete foundations and are joined with bolts and nails. Steel plates are used to strengthen the joints where the wooden parts meet.

A large number of parts make up a wooden coaster. For example, the American Eagle in Six Flags Great America, Gurnee, Illinois, used 2,000 concrete foundations; 1.6 million feet (487,000 meters) of wood; 60,720 bolts; and 30,600 pounds (13,910 kilograms) of nails; and 9,000 gallons (34,065 liters) of paint.

Steel coasters may use the same trestle-style supporting structures as those in wooden coasters. They may also use thick steel tubes for support. The tubular steel tracks are prefabricated, or manufactured in a factory, as large curved sections and later brought to the construction site for assembly. All steel surfaces are painted.

Like wooden coasters, steel coasters consist of numerous parts. For example, the Pepsi Max Big One coaster at Blackpool Pleasure Beach in Blackpool, England, used 1,270 piles driven into the sandy soil for the foundation; 2,215 tons (2,010 metric tons) of steel; and 60,000 bolts. The painted surfaces comprise 42,000 square yards (35,087 square meters).

The track and lift chain on both types of coasters are made of steel. The car bodies may be made of aluminum or fiberglass. The car wheels

lift hill: A steep hill with a linked chain or other mechanism that carries the roller coaster to the top. This hill is usually the first and highest on a roller coaster.

rails: Pairs of steel bars at the edges of tracks, just like those on a railroad track.

slammer: A sudden, hard drop that slams passengers down into their seats, giving riders a feeling of weightlessness.

track: The rails on which the roller coaster travels.

may be made of urethane or some other long-wearing, quiet-running material. The cars usually have steel axles (bars on which wheels turn) and substructures.

Design

The designers first determine what kind of riders will use the coaster. Children typically like coasters that are slow and have hills, drops, and curves that are gentle. On the opposite end are riders who enjoy being "scared to death," seeking out coasters that provide extreme speeds, heights, and turns. In between these two groups are those riders who, while wanting the sensational experience of a roller coaster ride, prefer moderate speeds and heights.

The designers have to decide how much ground and air spaces are needed for a particular roller coaster. They check out possible sites, as well as access roads, trees, lakes, and power lines. In cases where the amusement park has other rides or where the available space is small, designers have to figure out ways to fit the new roller coaster into the sur-roundings. Some coasters have been designed to thread their way through existing rides and walkways.

In a typical roller coaster, riders sit in cars. Steel construction has allowed for variations on this basic coaster ride. One model has passengers standing up instead of sitting down. Another type of coaster hangs from the track, giving the sensation of flying. This particular design, however, does not allow for inversion (part of the track that turns riders upside down) as it could be dangerous. Bobsled coasters have no track at all. Cars roll free in a chute, like a bobsled run.

Using a computer, the designers plan the arrangement of the hills, drops, and turns. The height of the first hill, or lift hill, must be calculated to give the cars enough energy to push them all the way through the ride and back to the station. A coaster does not have an engine to keep the cars going. It relies on the energy gathered as it climbs the lift hill.

The designers calculate the forces that the loaded cars exert on the tracks to ensure that the support structure is adequate. They also calculate the gravitational forces (also called g forces) exerted on the passengers at different points of the ride. Roller coasters are possible because of gravity, the force that pulls objects toward the earth. Gravitational forces, measured in g's, give people weight. The earth exerts a g force of 1 g when a person is standing on the ground. A person feels heavier when the g force is higher than 1 g and lighter when the g force is lower than 1 g.

When a roller coaster climbs uphill, the g force on the person increases, and his weight gets heavier. For example, if a person weighs 100 pounds (45.5 kilograms), a g force of 2 g's would exert 200 pounds (91 kilograms) of force on that person. In the United States, coasters generally exert no more than 3.5 g's, which is the limit that most people can take.

Next, the designers decide what features to add to make the particular roller coaster different from others. They may make the first climb higher or the speed of the lift chain slower to add excitement to the anticipated drop. The first drop is usually the highest and, therefore, the fastest and scariest. Other drops can be designed with a double dip, in which a hill has two separate drops by adding a short flattened section midway down the hill. Some drops, called slammers, have unexpected flat or upturned sections that slam passengers down into their seats.

The Manufacturing Process

Wooden roller coasters are usually constructed piece by piece in the amusement park. For steel roller coasters, the track sections are prefabricated in a factory, then transported to the site and put together. The following are the typical steps for manufacturing classic wooden coasters and modern steel coasters.

Preparing the construction site

1 The area where the roller coaster will be built has to be cleared and prepared. Roller coasters are usually built when the amusement park is closed for the season. If construction has to be done when the park is open, the area is fenced to keep people off the site.

2 Existing structures, vegetation, or utilities are removed or demolished. Any holes left are filled in with dirt.

3 The holes for the foundation of the support structure are laid out and then drilled or dug. Strong wooden forms (molds) are constructed to hold the concrete for the foundation points. If the soil is sandy, instead of concrete, large wooden columns may be driven into the ground to serve as foundations. Concrete is transported to the site in mixer trucks and pumped into the forms. Connector plates are imbedded

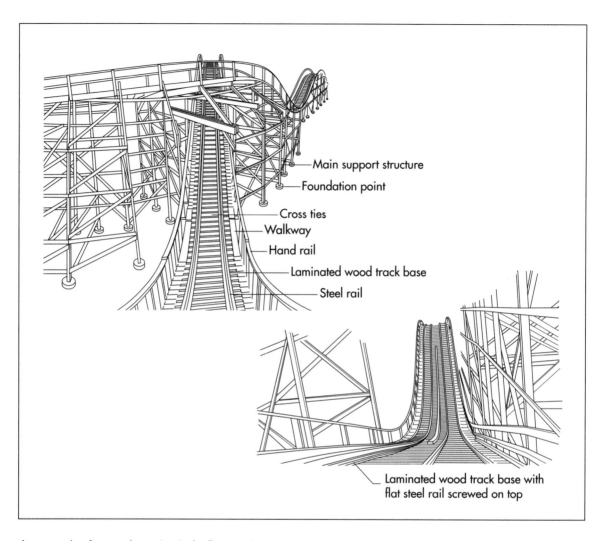

Main support structure

Foundation point

Cross ties

Walkway

Hand rail

Laminated wood track base

Steel rail

Laminated wood track base with
flat steel rail screwed on top

An example of a wood-constructed roller coaster.

into the concrete on top of the foundation so that supports can be attached
to the foundation.

Erecting the main support structure

4 After the foundation is laid, the main support structure is built. The supports, like the other parts of the steel coasters, are prefabricated. In the factory, the pieces for each support are cut and welded into the required shape. If a more complicated three-dimensional bend is required, a computer-controlled hydraulic (operated by water under pressure) tube bender is used.

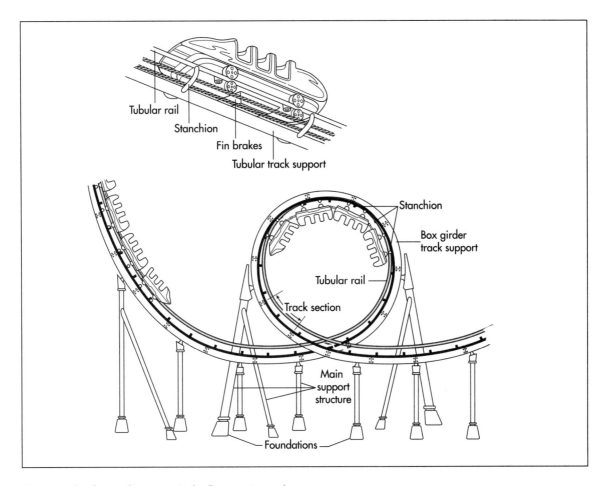

Tubular rail

Stanchion

Fin brakes

Tubular track support

Stanchion

Box girder track support

Tubular rail

Track section

Main support structure

Foundations

An example of a steel-constructed roller coaster and car.

To built the supports for wooden coasters, unfinished lumber is transported to the site, cut into pieces, and assembled. For both types of coasters, the lower portions of the main supports are lifted by a crane and attached to the connector plates on the foundation points.

5 The lower supports are temporarily braced (held steady by a framework) while the upper sections are attached. The work continues until the main support structure is complete.

Installing the track

6 On steel coasters, the track sections are manufactured in a factory with the stanchions (vertical supports) and tubular tracks welded to the track supports. At the site, the track sections are lifted into place, and the track ends are slid together. The sections are bolted to the main support structure and to each other.

On wooden coasters, wooden crosstie beams are placed across the top of the main support structures along the whole length of the ride. The base for the rails consists of six to eight layers of flat wooden boards bonded together and placed lengthwise in two rows on top of the crosstie beams. The rails themselves are formed from long, flat strips of steel screwed into the wooden base.

7 On steel coasters, walkways and handrails are welded in place along the outside of the track. This gives easy access for servicing the coaster and for emptying the ride of passengers in case of emergency. On wooden coasters, the parts of the crosstie beams outside of the tracks serve as walkways, and handrails are put in place.

8 The lift chain and anti-rollback mechanisms are installed on the lift hill. Unlike the brake system that is built into an automobile, the brake system of a roller coaster is built into the track and controlled by computers. Braking devices, located at the end of the track and at certain locations throughout the track, are installed.

Some of the more recent roller coasters are designed to have their riders' legs hanging from their seats, like the Mind Eraser at Six Flags Darien Lake theme park in Darien Center, New York. *Reproduced by permission of AP/Wide World Photos.*

Assembling the cars

9 The cars that are connected to make a train are made in the factory. The subframe pieces, or the pieces of the metal frame on which the car's body is built, are cut and welded. The bodies are stamped (cut

out by forcing into or against a mold) from aluminum or formed in fiberglass, then fastened to the subframes. The cushions may be cut from foam, mounted on a base, and covered with material.

Three kinds of wheels are used in the cars. The road wheels that sit on top of the track support the weight of the cars. Underneath the track are the upstop wheels, also called the underfriction wheels. They lock on to the cars, keeping them from jumping off the track. The third set of wheels called guide wheels inside and outside of the running rail "guide" a roller coaster along the path of the tracks. All these wheels are bolted in place with locking fasteners.

Other safety devices, including anti-rollback dogs and braking fins are also fitted under the cars. The anti-rollback dogs are the metal hooks that keep a climbing train from rolling backward by grasping the anti-rollbacks, or steel bars, on the track. In coasters that use a braking system consisting of fin brakes, a braking fin is attached to the bottom of the car. The fin-brake unit consists of two rectangular metal plates installed onto the track and the car braking fin, another rectangular plate. Computerized sensors on the track cause the fin brakes to "squeeze" the car braking fin, making the train of cars slow down or stop.

JOHN A. MILLER

John A. Miller (1874–1941) invented many of the safety devices that are still used in today's roller coasters. The underfriction wheels, also called the upstop wheels, allow the loops and steep climbs and dips that otherwise would not be possible because of the danger of the wheels leaping off the track. The safety chain dog, also called the anti-rollback dog, prevents the cars from rolling backward should the chain lift break. The clickety-clack sound riders hear when the cars go uphill is caused by this safety device.

Finishing the ride

10 After the main construction is finished, electrical wiring is installed for the lighting. The ride may be painted. The boarding station is constructed, and the signs and landscaping are added.

Quality Control

The design and construction of roller coasters are covered by government safety rules. The materials have to be strong enough to support the weight of the ride and riders. Government inspectors periodically inspect the various phases of the construction.

To make sure the ride is safe, the cars are filled with sandbags (to simulate the weight of riders) and sent through several rides around the entire track. The government investigators conduct a final check before allowing the ride to open to the public.

The Future

Higher, faster, and longer roller coasters continue to be built in the United States. Roller coasters have also become popular in other countries. The Dodonpa roller coaster in Fujikyu Highland, Japan, which opened in December 2001, has already surpassed Superman: The Escape as the fastest steel coaster in the world.

Designers may come up with more looping wooden coasters, which are not as easy to design as steel coasters. The Son of Beast coaster in Kings Mills, Ohio, is presently the only looping wooden coaster in the world. Opened in May 2000, it holds the worldwide record for the tallest (218 feet, or 66.4 meters) and fastest (78.4 miles per hour, or 126.2 kilometers per hour) wooden coaster.

Designers may introduce new designs of roller coasters called prototypes. In January 2002, the world's first four-dimensional coaster called X opened to the public at the Six Flags Magic Mountain in Valencia, California. The cars, which spin the riders 360 degrees forward and backward, are on an axis separate from the train's main movement. Designers of Thunderhawk, which opened on April 6, 2002, in Kansas City, Missouri, have incorporated several new features, including a fountain with computerized programs that will subject gondola riders to different degrees of soaking.

For More Information

Books

Bennett, David. *Roller Coaster: Wooden and Steel Coasters, Twisters, and Corkscrews.* Edison, NJ: Chartwell Books, 1998.

Cook, Nick. *Roller Coasters, or, I had So Much Fun, I Almost Puked.* Minneapolis, MN: Carolrhoda Books, Inc., 1998.

Throgmorton, Todd H. *Roller Coasters: United States and Canada.* 2nd ed. Jefferson, NC: McFarland & Company, Inc., 2000.

Web Sites

Harris, Tom. "How Roller Coasters Work." *How Stuff Works.* http://www.howstuffworks.com/roller-coaster.htm (accessed on June 24, 2002).

"Roller Coasters and Safety." *International Association of Amusement Parks and Attractions* http://www.iaapa.org/media/roll-sft.htm (accessed on June 24, 2002).

Satellite Dish

A satellite dish is a parabolic, or bowl-shaped, antenna that receives television signals from communications satellites that are circling the earth. Its main functions are to provide the viewer with a clear picture and a wide variety of channels. The dish can range from 18 inches (45.7 centimeters) to 10 feet (3 meters). According to the Satellite Industry Association, in 2001 about 80.7 million households worldwide had a home satellite system, bringing in estimated industry earnings of $3.12 billion.

A satellite dish is part of a satellite television system that consists of an uplink antenna at a broadcast station on Earth, a downlink antenna in the communications satellite in space, and numerous receiving satellite dishes. The satellite receives television signals from the station, amplifies them (increases their power), and sends them back to Earth. The television signals are in the form of microwaves, which are electromagnetic waves that travel at the speed of light (186,000 miles per second, or 299,274 kilometers per second).

According to the Satellite Industry Association, in 2001 about 80.7 million households worldwide had a home satellite system.

Visions of satellite broadcasting

In 1945, British science fiction writer and electronics engineer Arthur C. Clarke (1917–) suggested the use of three manned satellites to transmit communications signals all over the world. In "Extra-Terrestrial Relays: Can Rocket Stations Give World-Wide Radio Coverage?" (*Wireless World,*

October 1945), Clarke explained that the artificial satellites would be located above Earth's equator and that their twenty-four-hour orbit would coincide with Earth's rotation. This way, the satellites would be in a stationary, or fixed, position, allowing dish antennas that transmit and receive television signals to be pointed at the same spot in space.

Clarke was describing what more than two decades later became known as satellite broadcasting, the transmission of television and radio programs over a large part of the world. The communications satellites used for broadcasting are placed in an orbit, or path, about 22,300 miles (35,880 kilometers) above the equator. The orbit is called the "geostationary orbit" or the "geosynchronous orbit."

In the early 1950s, John R. Pierce (1910–), another science fiction writer and engineer with the Bell Telephone Laboratories, made calculations for sending microwave signals from one part of the world to another using communications satellites. Pierce's lecture on these calculations and the possible costs of such satellites were published in April 1955 ("Orbital Radio Relays," *Jet Propulsion*) At the time, he was unaware of Clarke's writing on geostationary communications satellite.

Visions fulfilled

On August 12, 1960, the United States launched *Echo 1*, the first communications satellite that transmitted telephone signals. John R. Pierce was one of the scientists involved in its design. Pierce and his colleagues at Bell Telephone Laboratories also developed *Telstar 1*, the first communications satellite to transmit television signals.

On July 10, 1962, live television pictures in the United States were seen in France courtesy of *Telstar 1*. Later that year, a second satellite, *Relay 1*, was put into orbit.

The first geosynchronous-orbit satellite, *Syncom 3*, was launched on August 19, 1964. Whereas *Telstar 1* provided less than two hours of television broadcast per day, *Syncom 3* transmitted twenty-four hours of live television because, being in a fixed spot above the equator, its orbit matched Earth's rotation. *Syncom 3* was always in the right position in relation to Earth, compared to *Telstar 1*, which was in the correct position only a few hours a day.

On June 25, 1967, during the first worldwide satellite television broadcast, the Beatles sang *All You Need Is Love* at BBC-TV in London, England. About 350,000 people watched the show.

artificial satellite: A manmade satellite, as compared to a natural satellite, such as the moon, which is Earth's satellite.

coaxial cable: A bundle of wires used for transmitting electrical signals at high speeds.

conduit: A tube that encloses and protects electrical cables.

downlink: The antenna on a communications satellite that beams television signals back to Earth.

electromagnetic wave: Wave of electrical and magnetic force produced by the vibration of electrons, the basic charges of electricity.

fiber optic cable: A bundle of hair-thin glass or plastic fibers that carry information as beams of light.

A view of *LEASAT Syncom-IV*, a communications satellite that malfunctioned shortly after it was put into orbit from the space shuttle *Discovery* in 1985. *Reproduced by permission of Corbis Corporation.*

Birth of the satellite television industry

In 1975, Home Box Office (HBO), a cable television company, started sending television programming to its affiliates in other parts of the country using satellite broadcasting. The following year, HBO introduced its satellite service. Other cable stations soon followed suit. The television stations used huge satellite dishes measuring about 33 feet (10 meters) in diameter to send signals into space. Communications satellites received the signals and, in turn, retransmitted them to satellite dishes in other parts of the United States or the world. The television programs reached consumers through coaxial cables. A coaxial cable is a thick bundle of wires that transmits electrical signals at high speeds.

First backyard dish

At around the same time, a Stanford University professor and National Aeronautics and Space Administration (NASA) scientist, H. Taylor Howard,

geostationary orbit: The path traveled by a communications satellite that keeps the satellite over the same place (22,250 miles, or 35,800 kilometers) above the equator and at the same speed as the earth's rotation. Also called geosynchronous orbit or Clarke Belt after Arthur C. Clarke.

designed the first satellite dish for personal use. The dish, placed into operation on September 14, 1976, was constructed of aluminum mesh and was about 16 feet (5 meters) in diameter. Overnight, the satellite dish industry grew, selling about five thousand home satellite systems at approximately $10,000 each.

Raw Materials

The basic satellite dish can be made from fiberglass (lightweight, strong material made from compressed glass fibers), PVC (polyvinyl chloride, a type of plastic), steel, solid aluminum, perforated (with tiny holes) aluminum, or wire mesh. Since fiberglass and PVC cannot reflect microwaves, a metallic surface is incorporated in the dish design (see below).

A steel feed horn and low noise amplifier/block downconverter (LNB) protrude from the center of the dish. The dish collects the incoming microwave signals from the satellite and concentrates them to the focal point of the dish. The feed horn, located at the focal point, collects the signals and directs them to the LNB. By the time the microwave signals reach the dish, they are rather weak. The LNB, which is the actual antenna, amplifies (increases the power of) the microwave signals and converts them to electrical signals, which travel by fiber optic cable to a receiver inside the home.

The steel actuator consists of the motor and gear assembly, the mechanism that enables the dish to receive signals from more than one satellite. There are two types of actuators. The horizon-to-horizon actuator, which is situated at the fulcrum of the dish, tracks satellites between the east and west horizon. The linear actuator, which attaches to the dish at one end and to the mount on the other end, has a more limited scope.

The Manufacturing Process

Satellite dishes can be made from different materials, using any one of several manufacturing processes. The dishes must have a metal on their surface in order to reflect microwaves.

Making the dish

inclinometer: An instrument that measures angles.

latitude: Location on the earth's surface north or south of the equator and measured in degrees of angle.

orbit: The path of a manmade satellite circling the earth.

uplink: An antenna on the ground that transmits television signals to a communications satellite.

1 If fiberglass is used to make the satellite dish, a reflective surface is included in the design because fiberglass does not reflect microwaves. First, a compound paste is made from a metallic mater-

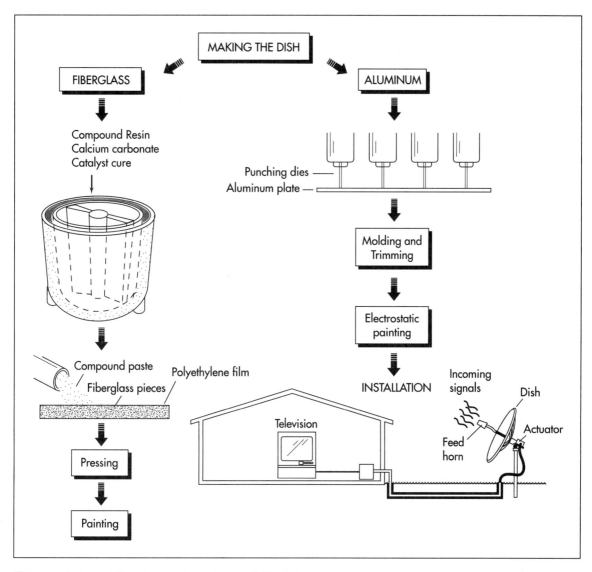

The manufacture of fiberglass and aluminum satellite dishes.

ial mixed with polyester resin, calcium carbonate, and catalyst cure. The paste is poured onto a sheet of polyethylene film that has chopped fiberglass fibers added. The result is a sheet layered with the compound paste, fiberglass, and polyethylene film.

The sheet is pressed at 89 degrees Fahrenheit (30 degrees Celsius) to set the layers. To shape the sheet into the desired parabolic (bowl-like) form, it is subjected to a high pressure of 1,544 to 2,426 tons (1,400 to 2,200

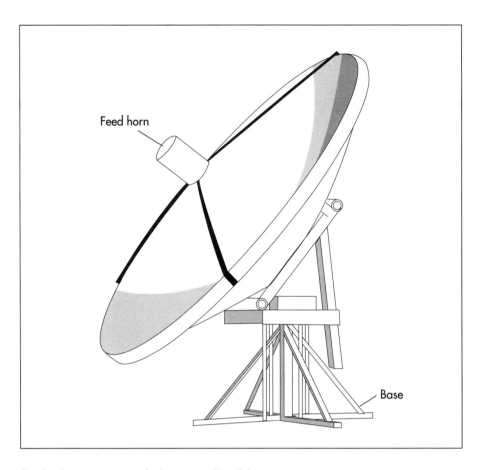

Feed horn

Base

The basic components of a home satellite dish.

metric tons). The dish is trimmed, cooled, and painted. After the paint has dried, the dish is packed in sturdy boxes for shipping.

2   If aluminum is used to make the satellite dish, the aluminum plate is perforated with a punching die (mold), creating tiny holes. The plate is then heated, stretched over a form, cooled, and trimmed. For protection, a paint powder coating is applied to the plate using an electrostatic charge. The paint is given an opposite electrical charge from the plate, so that it sticks to the plate.

3   A satellite dish may also be made from wire-mesh petals consisting of fine holes. The petals are made from aluminum that is extruded, or formed by forcing it into a die of the desired shape. They are usually joined together on site by sliding them into aluminum ribs that attach

to the hub (central part of the dish). The petals are then secured to the ribs with metal clips.

Installation

4 All completed satellite dishes will have the necessary equipment (the feed horn, the amplifier) installed in the factory. The dish can be set up either by a professional installer or by the buyer. The method of installation depends on the size of the dish and the mechanical expertise of the buyer.

The installation site should be reasonably clear of obstructions and not more than 246 feet (75 meters) from the house. The buyer has to follow the local building codes and find out where underground utility lines may be buried so as not to accidentally cut these lines. The buyer must also be aware of the possibility of microwave interference from radio and television towers in the area.

5 Once the site is selected, the foundation is installed. It may be a pole-type foundation or a slab foundation. A pole-type foundation is usually used for satellite dishes no larger than 12 feet (3.7 meters) in diameter. It consists of a steel, tube-like pole set into a concrete base that extends below the frost line (the point below the earth's surface beyond which freezing does not occur).

A hole four times the diameter of the pole is dug for the base. About 6 inches (15.2 centimeters) of gravel (for drainage) is added to the bottom of the hole, and the pole is positioned above the gravel. The standard ground pole generally measures 5 feet (1.5 meters) above ground and extends 3 feet (1 meter) underground. For longer poles, installers add additional lengths to the section underground and widen the hole around the pole. Some installers fit the pole bottom with two metal bars at a right angle to each other, which are either drilled through the pole or welded to it. The metal bars keep the pole from twisting in its foundation when strong wind acts on the dish.

Before concrete is poured, a trench is dug for the coaxial cables that connect the satellite dish to the electronics located near the television. The cables are enclosed in a conduit, a pipe made of aluminum or gray PVC (polyvinyl chloride, known for its resistance to moisture and weathering). Part of the conduit leaves the trench and extends into the concrete hole and stands parallel to the support pole, where it is clamped in place. Finally, a weatherhead (a cap) is used to cover the open end of the conduit. Then, concrete is poured into the pole and into the hole around it.

A satellite dish sits on the roof of a house. *Photograph by Kelly A. Quin. Copyright © Kelly A. Quin. Reproduced by permission of the photographer.*

A slab foundation is recommended in rocky or sandy areas, or if the satellite dish is larger than 12 feet (3.7 meters) in diameter. The slab foundation is built by digging to the proper depth. The length and width of the slab should be at least half the diameter of the satellite dish. Gravel is added, and a wooden form is put in place to hold the poured concrete. A wire mesh may be spread over the slab area to strengthen the finished concrete. As with the post-type foundation, the coaxial cables are encased in a conduit before the concrete is poured. After pouring the concrete, a triangular steel fixture for mounting is embedded into the slab.

6 The mount, which supports the dish, is attached to either the pole or the triangular steel fixture. The elevation arm, which rotates the dish, is then attached to the pedestal.

Alignment

7 The mounted satellite dish must be aligned in order to point toward the communications satellite. This is typically done by a professional who uses instruments, such as an inclinometer, to measure the

angle at which the dish faces the satellite. The angle at which the dish is eventually situated will vary according to which satellite is selected and at what latitude the dish is located. The latitude pertains to the location of the dish installation site on the earth's surface north or south of the equator.

Quality Control

Satellite dishes manufactured for consumers do not undergo strict tests, although certain requirements have to be met. If the aluminum dish has a perforated design or consists of wire mesh petals, the holes must be relatively small to minimize signal loss. To ensure that the microwaves are received properly, the dish surface has to be very smooth, the parabolic shape has to be exact, and the curvature has to be very accurate. Even small imperfections on the dish surface, or dents, can cause loss of signals. A reflective surface is needed to reflect the microwaves; therefore, metal is a necessary component of the dish surface. The pole support has to be constructed so that it can withstand strong winds. The mount should be sturdy and attached securely to the dish and the supporting structures. The dish must be aligned properly for maximum signal reception.

MICROWAVES AND SATELLITES

Microwaves are very short electromagnetic waves created by the vibration of electrons. Microwaves, the same ones used in microwave ovens, are ideal for transmitting television signals. They are capable of transmitting a lot of information and at a very high speed. Microwaves can also be concentrated into a very powerful beam, which comes in handy when a dish antenna on Earth aims those waves toward a communications satellite. In addition, microwaves are not affected by noises in the atmosphere, and can pass through the upper atmosphere into space with no difficulty.

After the dish is installed, the owner is generally responsible for cleaning it when necessary, as well as tightening and lubricating all bolts. The owner is also responsible for trimming any obstructive vegetation around the dish. Heavy winds may sometimes push the dish out of alignment, so that it is no longer properly aimed at the satellite. In this case, realignment has to be performed.

The Future

As more powerful satellites are launched in the geosynchronous orbit, satellite dishes as small as 18 inches (46 centimeters; called minidishes) in diameter are able to receive television signals. Most of these dishes are easily mounted on rooftops and window sills.

The direct-to-home broadcast television programming that uses the minidish continues to develop. In 2001, about eight million Americans had direct-to-home broadcast television, more than doubling the 1995 figure (3.5 million subscribers). The system offers more than two hundred program channels. In addition, the system uses digital transmission, the same technology used in computers, which means laser-disk-quality pictures and sounds. A new trend involves the installation of the small satellite dish in recreational vehicles and trucks.

Satellite dishes can now help consumers, especially those in rural areas who have previously relied on slow dial-up connections, to obtain high-speed Internet access. In 2001, satellite dish television companies started offering such a service, enabling Internet users to receive and send data by satellite. The new technology is more expensive than the traditional cable and DSL (Digital Subscriber Lines) connections, but some consumers are using the same service to access satellite television programming. Industry experts predict that, as with the cost of the home satellite system, the price of this technology will go down over time.

For More Information

Books

Long, Mark. *The World of Satellite Television.* 9th ed. Summertown, TN: The Book Publishing Company, 1998.

Ross, John A. *Howard W. Sams Guide to Satellite TV Technology.* Indianapolis, IN: Prompt Publications, 1999.

Periodicals

"Broadband From Above: Satellite Services Beam High-Speed Access Anywhere." *PC World.* (February 2001): p. 64.

"A Wider Orbit: Where Cable and DSL Don't Go, Satellite Internet Access Does—for a Price." *The Dallas Morning News.* (January 24, 2002): p. 3D.

Web Sites

Boeing Satellite Systems, Inc. "What Is a Satellite?" *Satellite Industry Association.* http://www.sia.org/papers/sat101.pdf (accessed on July 22, 2002).

"Communications Satellites: Making the Global Village Possible." *National Aeronautics and Space Administration.* http://www.hq.nasa.gov/office/pao/History/satcomhistory.html (accessed July 22, 2002).

"Satellite Industry Key Dates." *Satellite Broadcasting and Communications Association.* http://www.sbca.com/key_dates.html (accessed July 22, 2002).

Skyscraper

Reproduced by permission of Corbis Corporation.

A skyscraper is a very tall building with many stories. Skyscrapers usually refer to structures that serve as residences or work places for thousands of people. The term "skyscraper" was first used in the United States in the 1880s, where the form of the structure originated. Originally used to describe a building with at least ten stories, today it refers to buildings with forty to more than one hundred floors. Its height is measured from the street level where the main entrance is located to the top of the structure, which includes spires (the tapered portion on top of a building's roof). However flagpoles, television antennas, and radio antennas are not included.

The tallest skyscrapers in the world are a pair of office buildings in Kuala Lumpur, Malaysia. The Petronas Twin Towers stand 1,483 feet (452 meters) tall, including spires. Completed in 1997, each of the towers holds eighty-eight stories. The Sears Tower in Chicago, Illinois, at 1,454 feet (443 meters), is the second tallest skyscraper. It opened in 1974. (The television antenna on top of the 110-story building adds an additional 253 feet [77 meters] to its height.) The third tallest skyscraper, the Jin Mao Tower in Shanghai, China, rises to 1,381 feet (421 meters). It was constructed in 1998 and has eighty-eight stories.

The Empire State Building in New York, New York, completed in 1931, held the title of the world's tallest skyscraper for more than forty years. In 1972, the twin towers of the World Trade Center surpassed the Empire State Building in height. The twin towers, which collapsed due to damage

The ten-story Home Insurance Company Building, built in Chicago, Illinois, in 1885, is considered to be the first modern skyscraper.

235

The Petronas Towers, in Kuala Lumpur, Malaysia. At 1,483 feet (452 meters), the twin towers are the tallest buildings in the world. *Reproduced by permission of AP/Wide World Photos.*

sustained from a terrorist attack on September 11, 2001, each had 110 floors and rose to 1,362 feet (415 meters) and 1,368 (417 meters), respectively.

Building up instead of out

During the 1850s, the need for more office spaces in big cities, where land was expensive or scarce, gave rise to the construction of buildings that could hold several stories. The walls of a building typically support its structure; therefore, a tall building would require very thick stone or brick walls on the lower stories to hold up the higher levels. The earliest tall buildings in the United States consisted of about five stories, with the lower floors losing plenty of space to the thick walls. In later years, architects used cast iron (a metal composed of a mixture of iron, carbon, and silicon) frames to bear the weight of the upper floors. The walls remained of stone and brick construction.

Rising to new heights

In the late 1880s, major technological advances made possible the design and construction of buildings with more stories. The invention of steel-frame construction, in which a rigid steel skeleton supported the building's weight, eliminated the need for very thick walls. The outer walls, made of bricks or stones, held only their own weight and were then supported by the steel frame. The first skyscraper to use this design was the ten-story Home Insurance Company Building, which was built in Chicago, Illinois, in 1885 by William Le Baron Jenney (1832–1907). This was considered the first skyscraper.

Steel (an alloy of iron and carbon), being stronger and weighing less than iron, was the ideal material for the framework because it allowed for additional stories. The ability to mass-produce steel further increased the construction of skyscrapers.

The invention of the safety elevator in 1852 by Elisha Otis (1811–1861) created the ability to reach the upper stories of tall buildings with ease and safety. This steam-powered rope elevator had an automatic safety device that kept it from falling if the lifting rope broke. Nearly forty years later, in 1889, the high-speed, electric-powered, roped elevator enabled the construction of higher structures.

Raw Materials

Reinforced concrete is an important component (part) of skyscrapers. It is made from concrete poured around a framework of steel rods,

alloy: A mixture of a metal and a nonmetal or a mixture of two or more metals. For example, steel is an alloy made of the metal iron and the nonmetal carbon. Brass is an alloy made of two metals, copper and zinc.

architect: A person who designs a building, determining the shape and height as well as its inside and outside appearances.

beam: Horizontal piece of a frame.

bolt: A threaded metal pin with a head. It is inserted through a hole in a building piece and is secured with a nut. The nut, a small piece of metal, has a threaded hole that fits around the bolt to keep it in place.

cladding: Material that makes up the exterior wall of a skyscraper.

column: Vertical piece of a frame.

Some of the world's tallest structures are not necessarily skyscrapers because they do not house offices or living quarters. The world's tallest freestanding (standing unsupported or with attachment) structure is not a skyscraper. The CN tower in Toronto, Canada, was erected in 1975 to support a huge television antenna. It measures 1,815 feet (553 meters), with the Skypod (comprised of a restaurant, nightclub, and an observation viewing deck) at around 1,100 feet (335 meters) from the street. The world's second largest freestanding structure is also a television tower that was built in 1967. The Ostankino Tower in Moscow, Russia, has an observation deck located almost two-thirds up the tower's total height of 1,771 feet (540 meters). A restaurant called the Seventh Heaven, with three dining areas, is located below the observation deck.

concrete: A mixture of cement powder, water, gravel, and sand.

strengthening the resulting dried concrete against bending movement caused by the wind. A type of high-strength concrete has been developed by adding very fine particles to the regular concrete ingredients. The increased surface area of these tiny particles produces a stronger bond. This type of concrete was used in Petronas Twin Towers.

The other important material for skyscraper construction is steel. Different sizes of steel beams (long pieces of steel) are delivered to the construction site as they are needed. Before delivery, the beams are coated with a substance that protects them from rust and heat. After each beam is welded into place, the same coating substance is used to cover the fresh joints. Another layer of insulation, such as fiberglass batting covered with aluminum foil, may then be wrapped around the beams.

The exterior walls of a skyscraper are called curtain walls because they hang from the frames like curtains. A variety of materials, called claddings, make up these exterior walls. They may be glass; metal, such as aluminum or stainless steel; or masonry materials, such as granite, marble, or limestone.

Design

The architect designs the skyscraper, determining the shape and height as well as its inside and outside appearances. Some architects use a computer program that helps them see how the skyscraper will look when completed, or how the building will fit into its surroundings.

Next, structural engineers put the architect's ideas into a detailed plan. The engineers make sure the structure will support not only the weight of the skyscraper, but also the weight of the people and furniture the skyscraper will contain.

Tall buildings, especially their top levels, can sway anywhere from two inches to more than two feet in strong winds. The engineers have to make sure the structure is sound enough that it will not be toppled by the sideways force of wind, or that it will not sway too much to cause the

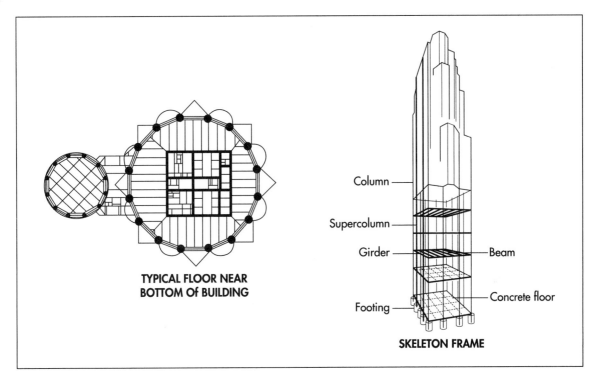

An example of a skyscraper ground floor and building frame. The square in the ground floor is the core space.

occupants physical or emotional discomfort. Models of the planned building are tested in wind tunnels to determine the effects of high winds.

If tests show the building will sway excessively in strong winds, designers may add a central core. They may also incorporate devices to counteract the motion or restrict motion. One such device is called the tuned mass damper, which is a heavy weight in the top level of the building. When the building starts to sway, the computer system moves this heavy weight in the opposite direction, thereby reducing the amount of sway.

Tall buildings also affect the wind patterns of surrounding areas. The wind between skyscrapers that are built near one another is known to be stronger.

Each skyscraper design is different. Major structural designs that may be used alone or combined with others include a steel skeleton hidden behind curtain walls that do not support the structure's weight and a reinforced concrete skeleton that is in-filled with cladding panels to form

corrugated steel: A steel sheet, shaped into folds for rigidity.

masonry: Stonework or brickwork.

reinforced concrete: Concrete that is made stronger by having steel rods embedded in it.

spire: The tapered portion on top of a building's roof.

exterior walls. The design may also include a central concrete core to hold the elevators, as well as the air conditioning, water pipes, and ducts for electrical wirings. Still another design includes support columns around the perimeter of the building that are connected by horizontal beams to one another and to the core.

The Construction Process

Each skyscraper is designed to suit the needs of its future occupants, whether they are apartment dwellers or office workers. The owner and the architect have to approve what the final structure will look like. The structure of the building also has to take into consideration the layout of the land and the type of climate in the area. For example, in Japan, designers have to allow for the occurrence of earthquakes when they design the structure. The construction process for each building differs. However, all skyscrapers follow basic methods.

The substructure

1 Construction usually begins with digging a hole that will hold the foundation. The depth of the hole depends on how far down the bedrock (solid rock deep underground) is and how many basement levels will be built.

Digging a deep hole can cause movement of the surrounding soil. To prevent this from happening and to seal out water from around the foundation site, a diaphragm wall is constructed. This is done by digging a deep narrow ditch around the boundary of the planned hole. As the ditch is dug, it is filled with slurry (watery clay) to keep its sides from collapsing. As each section of the ditch reaches the desired depth, a cage of reinforced steel is lowered into it. Concrete is pumped into the ditch, displacing the slurry. The slurry is reused in other sections of the ditch. The concrete hardens, forming the wall.

2 If the bedrock lies close to the surface, the soil on top of it is removed. The bedrock surface is smoothed to form a leveled surface for the foundation. Footings (holes into which the building's support columns will be held in place) are drilled in the bedrock. Then the support columns made of steel or reinforced concrete are placed in the footings.

weld: To unite metal pieces by applying heat, which melts the edges of the pieces, joining them together.

3 If the bedrock lies very deep, long steel columns or reinforced concrete columns called piles are sunk through the soil until they are embedded in the bedrock. This can be done using one of two methods. Steel piles may be embedded in the bedrock by repeatedly dropping

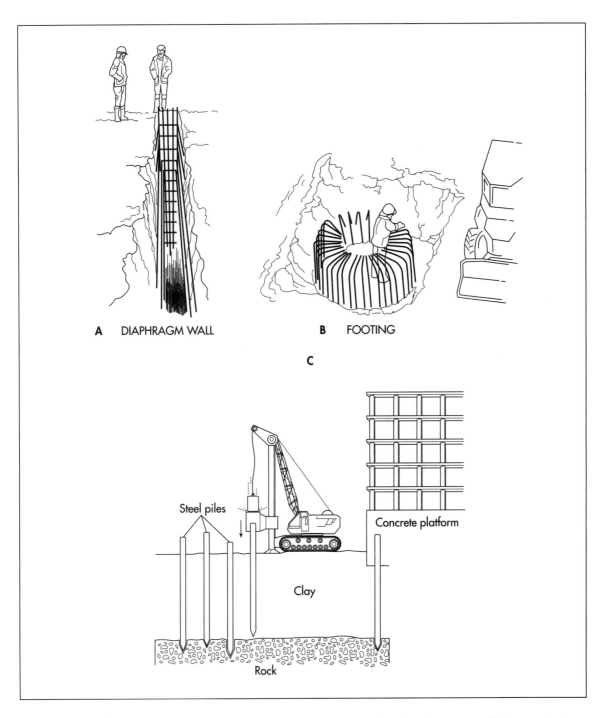

A DIAPHRAGM WALL

B FOOTING

C

Steel piles

Concrete platform

Clay

Rock

Examples of (A) diaphragm wall, (B) footing, and (C) one type of foundation for a skyscraper, which uses steel piles to secure the foundation to the ground.

a heavy weight on their tops. The second method involves drilling shafts (large tubes) through the soil and into the bedrock. Steel rods are inserted through the shafts and concrete is poured around them, resulting in reinforced concrete columns.

4 Finally, a foundation platform of reinforced concrete is poured on top of the support columns.

The superstructure and core

Once construction of a skyscraper has started, work on several phases of the structure generally takes place at the same time. For example, when the support columns are several stories high, workers begin building floors for the lower stories. As the columns are built higher, the flooring crews move to higher stories. In the meantime, the finishing crews start work on the lowest level. This process not only saves time but also ensures that the structure stays safe during construction.

5 If steel columns and beams are used in the building, each piece is lifted into place by tall cranes (machines that lift and move heavy materials). While the lowest stories are under construction, the cranes stay on the ground. As the structure rises higher, the cranes may be placed on the highest completed level of the steel skeleton.

Workers either bolt or weld the ends of the beams into place.

6 Many skyscrapers have a core (middle section) made of concrete. The core serves to keep the structure from swaying too much from strong winds. The core usually contains the elevator shafts, as well as the pipes for transporting water and the ducts (large pipes) for electrical wirings. Concrete may also be used to construct support columns.

Concrete cores and support columns are constructed using a technique called slip-forming. Steel rods are put inside a metal or wooden form called a formwork, which is made to the desired shape. The formwork is constructed so that it moves upward. As concrete is poured around the rods inside the formwork, the formwork rises. The speed of the climbing formwork is timed so that the concrete at the lower part has set before the formwork moves upward. The concrete mixture has to be such that it has hardened by the time the formwork is raised. In this way, the entire concrete core or column is made as one continuous piece.

7 In some skyscrapers, the floors are made of reinforced concrete. In others, the floors are supported by horizontal steel beams that are attached to the core and/or support columns. Steel decks (panels of

A crane is positioned next to a skyscraper under construction. *Reproduced by permission of Corbis Corporation.*

thin, corrugated steel) are laid on the beams and welded in place. Then, concrete is poured over the steel decks.

The exterior

8 In most skyscrapers, the core and support columns bear the weight of the structure and its contents. The outer walls simply enclose the structure. The walls are constructed by attaching panels of materials, such as glass, metal, and stone, to the building's framework. These materials are called claddings.

Finishing

9 After a story has been enclosed by exterior walls, it is ready for interior finishing. This includes installation of electrical wires, telephone wires, plumbing pipes, interior walls, ceiling panels, bathroom fixtures, lighting fixtures, water tanks, and sprinkler systems for fire control. Mechanical components, such as elevators, air conditioners, heating systems, and electricity generators are also put in place.

10 After completion of the superstructure, a roof is installed. This may be constructed like a floor and then waterproofed with a layer of rubber or plastic. Finally, the roof is covered with attractive weather-resistant tiles or metal.

The Future

The race is always on for constructing the highest skyscraper. The building at 7 South Dearborn Street in Chicago, Illinois, due for completion by 2004, will surpass the Petronas Twin Towers. It will rise 1,550 feet (471 meters) and contain 108 stories. Two television antennas will make the total height 2,000 feet.

Plans for other skyscrapers are being developed. In India, two pyramid-shaped buildings are being proposed. The taller of the two would reach 2,222 feet (677 meters). Japan, faced with scarce land to house its growing population, has proposed the X-Seed 4000, its name designating its height in meters. The 12,000-foot building is designed to accommodate about one million people. Another idea involves a skyscraper called the Millennium Tower (2,438 feet, or 800 meters) to be constructed in the Bay of Tokyo.

While building these skyscrapers is possible, they are just ideas. Such projects would cost a lot of money because extremely tall structures require very strong foundations and materials. The task of getting materials up to the highest stories would also require more expenses. Additional stories would require more elevators that would take up more spaces in the building core. One solution is to group passengers according to a common destination. Another solution is to have two sets of elevators—one elevator to take passengers partway up the building and another elevator to take these passengers the rest of the way.

For More Information

Books

Macaulay, David. *Building Big*. Boston, MA: Houghton Mifflin Company, 2000.

Oxlade, Chris. *Skyscrapers*. Chicago, IL: Reed Educational & Professional Publishing, 2001.

Severance, John B. *Skyscrapers: How America Grew Up*. New York, NY: Holiday House, 2000.

Web Sites

Harris, Tom. "How Skyscrapers Work." *How Stuff Works.*
http://howstuffworks.com/skyscraper.htm (accessed on July 22, 2002).

The Skyscraper Museum. http://www.skyscraper.org (accessed July 22, 2002).

SkyscraperPage.com. http://www.skyscraperpage.com (accessed July 22, 2002).

Soft Drink

Photograph by Kelly A. Quin. Copyright © Kelly A. Quin. Reproduced by permission of the photographer.

The term "soda pop" was coined in 1861 from the popping sound of escaping gas as a soda bottle was opened.

A soft drink is a nonalcoholic beverage consisting primarily of carbonated (with carbon dioxide gas added) water, sweetener, and flavorings. A soft drink may be a cola, ginger ale, ginger beer, root beer, or a fruit-flavored beverage. It is sold in bottles and cans or dispensed by a soda fountain into a glass. The name "soft drink" has been adopted to distinguish it from "hard drinks," or alcoholic beverages.

Soft drinks account for one of every four beverages consumed in the United States. According to the National Soft Drink Association, Americans drink an average of fifty-four gallons of soft drinks per person a year.

Bubble bath

The roots of soft drinks can be traced to ancient times. About two thousand years ago, Greeks and Romans recognized the medicinal value of mineral water and bathed in it for relaxation, a practice that continues today. Mineral water is spring water containing mineral salts and gases. One of the gases is carbon dioxide, later an important ingredient in soft drinks.

Starting around the 1300s, Europeans bathed in natural springs for their curative benefits. Some of the springs produced bubbles, which scientists concluded was due to the carbon dioxide gas dissolved in them. The American Indians were using "medicinal waters" long before the first colonists arrived in the United States.

Manmade mineral water

In 1767, British chemist Joseph Priestley (1733–1804) made the first carbonated water by adding water to carbon dioxide gas from fermented beer. Shortly after, Swedish chemist Torbern Bergman (1735–1784) invented a device that produced large quantities of mineral water from chalk. By the late 1700s, Europeans and Americans were drinking the sparkling mineral water for their health. In 1798, the term "soda water" was first used to refer to the manmade mineral water. In the United States, the first manmade soda water was patented in 1809. It consisted of water and sodium bicarbonate mixed with acid to produce gas bubbles.

Pharmacists in the United States and Europe, who sold most of the soda water, experimented with many ingredients in the hope of finding new remedies. These included dandelion, birch bark, sarsaparilla roots, and raspberry and strawberry leaves. Some pharmacists used fruit extracts of lemons and oranges, while those who were also chemists invented artificial colors and flavors. Before long, people were buying soda water just for its refreshing taste. Starting in the early 1800s, drug store soda fountains became popular gathering places for the local people. The market expanded in the 1830s when soda water was first sold in glass bottles. In 1850, the invention of a filling and corking machine solved the problem of capping the gaseous bottles. Unlike the Crown Soda Machine (see sidebar on page 249), the device called for a two-step filling, first with syrup, and then with carbonated water.

Caffeinated soda water

In 1886, a Georgia pharmacist, John Pemberton (1831–1888), created what would become the world's most famous drink, Coca-Cola™. Originally advertised as a medicinal beverage, his recipe included, among other ingredients, the extracts of the known stimulants coca leaves and cola nuts. In 1898, Caleb Bradham (1867–1934) of North Carolina invented Pepsi-Cola, named after cola nuts and pepsin, an acid that aids in digestion. However, Bradham did not advertise his product as a curative beverage. By the early twentieth century, like Bradham, most cola companies advertised their products not as medicines but as refreshments.

Growing thirst

The rapid popularity of the newly invented automobiles in the early 1900s contributed to the growth of the soft drink industry. Vending

activated charcoal: Carbon in powder or granular form which can be used as a filter by collecting impurities on its surface.

caffeine: The stimulant found in coffee, tea, cocoa, and the cola nuts used in soft drinks.

carbonated water: A bubbly water that is filled with carbon dioxide gas under pressure used to make soft drinks.

carbon dioxide: A natural gas that is dissolved in water to make carbonated water.

emulsion: A mixture of liquids that do not dissolve in each other; for example, oil and water.

extract: A concentrated form of the essential parts of a flavoring, food, or other substance.

flash pasteurization: The quick heating and cooling of a substance to kill harmful microorganisms.

An old-fashioned soda fountain, circa 1905. *Reproduced by permission of Corbis Corporation.*

franchise:
Authorization given
by a manufacturer
to a company or
companies to sell
his or her products
in a certain area.

gum: A sticky
substance found in
some trees and
plants.

mouthfeel:
Physical sensation
of food in the
mouth.

machines, dispensing soft drinks in cups, became regular fixtures at the service stations starting in the early 1920s. In the mid-1960s, for the first time, Coca-Cola and Pepsi-Cola were sold in all-aluminum cans, equipped with pull-ring tabs and later with stay-on tabs (created in 1974). In 1970, plastic bottles were used for soft drinks. Although another type of plastic called PET (polyethylene terephthalate) was invented in 1973, the soft drink industry did not use it in large quantities until 1991.

Soft drink companies are constantly on the lookout for consumer preferences. In the 1950s, after the sales of Pepsi-Cola rose when its sugar content was reduced, the first no-cal (calorie) beverages using the artificial sweetener saccharin were introduced. Since then, other new products have been introduced. They include diet, caffeine-free, low-sodium, and preservative-free drinks. Clear colas, as well as soft drinks with a lemon twist, have also been developed.

Raw Materials

A soft drink is made up of about 94 percent carbonated water. Carbon dioxide adds that special sparkle and bite to the beverage. It also acts as a

ONE MAN'S PRACTICAL INVENTIONS

Two inventions during the early years of the soft drink industry helped perfect the bottling of carbonated beverages for home use. In 1892, William Painter (1838–1906) invented the Crown Cork Cap, a metal cap with corrugated edges that gripped the neck of the bottle. Inside the cap was a thin piece of cork and a special paper that sealed the bottle and prevented the soft drink from coming in contact with the metal cap. Previously, the numerous bottle caps that had been introduced were not tight enough so that the soft drinks leaked or the carbon dioxide gas escaped from the bottle. Also, bottled drinks tended to change in taste and color after coming in contact with the metal caps.

In 1898, Painter invented the Crown Soda Machine, which filled and capped bottles at the same time. The machine consisted of a carbonated water line and a syrup line that fed the ingredients into one opening, so that the beverage came out of the machine already mixed. A bottle was filled, and then a press (a machine that uses pressure) on which a Crown Cork Cap had been placed crimped the cap over the bottle top, sealing it tightly. The first machine to incorporate the ingredients in a single step, Painter's invention is the ancestor of today's automated machines for bottling soft drinks.

mild preservative. Carbon dioxide is an inactive (does not react with other substances), colorless, and odorless natural gas. It is nonpoisonous, relatively inexpensive, and easy to liquefy (to cause to become liquid). The hissing sound and small bubbles resulting from the opening of a soft drink container are caused by the escape of carbon dioxide when pressure in the can is released.

Sugar, the second main ingredient, makes up 7 to 14 percent of a regular (nondiet) soft drink. Used in either dry or liquid form, sugar adds sweetness and body to the beverage, increasing the mouthfeel (physical sensation of food in the mouth), an important part of consumer enjoyment of a soft drink. Sucrose (made from sugar cane or sugar beets), high fructose corn syrup (made from cornstarch), or a combination of both sweeteners may be used.

Diet, or sugar-free, soft drinks use sugar substitutes, also called "diet" or "low-calorie" sweeteners. They include aspartame, saccharin, sucralose, and acesulfame-K (acesulfame potassium). A soft drink may use one sugar substitute or a combination of sugar substitutes.

Acids are added to soft drinks to give them a pleasant sharpness and to quench the thirst by stimulating saliva flow. They also act as a preserv-

pectin: A substance found in the rind of citrus and other fruits.

pH: A measure of the acidity of a liquid or solution.

polyethylene terephthalate (PET): A type of plastic used for packaging food and nonfood products. It is lightweight, inexpensive, break-resistant, and recyclable.

A soda dispenser is a common sight at fast-food restaurants and cafeterias. *Photograph by Kelly A. Quin. Copyright © Kelly A. Quin. Reproduced by permission of the photographer.*

ative. The most commonly used acids are citric acid, which gives a lemony flavor, and phosphoric acid. Other acids, such as malic acid or tartaric acid, may also be used.

Flavoring is a very important ingredient in soft drinks. Natural flavors come from natural extracts and oils, as well as spices. For example, an orange-flavored soft drink typically contains an orange extract. Root beer and ginger ale use flavors made from spices and herbs. Some soft drinks may use artificial, or manmade, flavorings.

Small amounts of other ingredients are added to soft drinks. Caffeine, one of the ingredients added to cola- and pepper-type soft drinks first introduced in the 1800s, is still used to enhance the flavorings used. Emulsions, consisting of water and such substances as gums and pectins, add to the "eye appeal" by acting as clouding agents. In beverages, such as cream soda, ginger beer, and root beer, saponin is added to produce a foam. Color used in soft drinks may come from natural or artificial color or a combination of both. Preservatives, including the antioxidants BHA and ascorbic acid, are used to maintain the taste, color, and flavor of the beverages.

saponin: A plant substance that forms a foam and is used in such soft drinks as root beer.

shelf life: The length of time a product may be stored before it starts losing its freshness.

The Manufacturing Process

Most soft drinks are generally produced at local bottling and canning companies. A soft drink manufacturer grants a company or companies a franchise (the authorization to sell his or her products in a certain area). That franchise company in turn grants a license (an official permission) to a bottling or canning company to mix the soft drink strictly following the secret formula and manufacturing procedures.

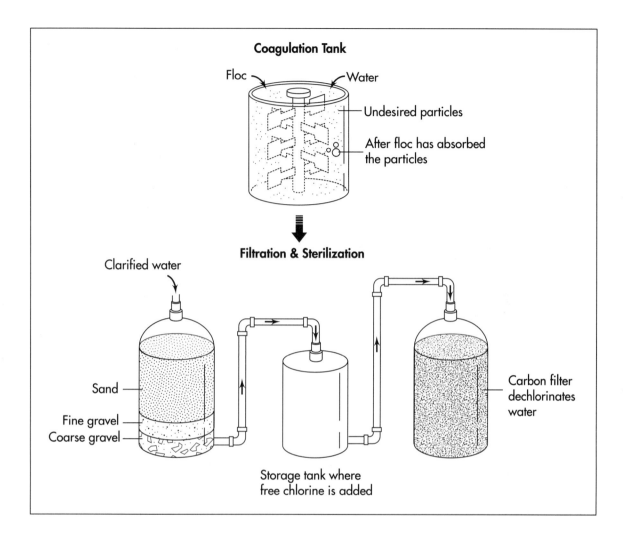

Coagulation Tank

Floc

Water

Undesired particles

After floc has absorbed the particles

Filtration & Sterilization

Clarified water

Sand

Fine gravel

Coarse gravel

Storage tank where free chlorine is added

Carbon filter dechlorinates water

Clarifying the water

1   A regular soft drink contains about 90 percent water, while a diet soft drink can have as much as 99 percent water. Impurities, such as suspended particles, organic matter (the remains of living things), and bacteria may diminish the quality of the taste and color of the soft drink. Impurities are removed through a series of coagulation, filtration, and chlorination processes.

During coagulation, a gelatinous precipitate, or floc (ferric sulphate or aluminum sulphate), is mixed into the water. The floc absorbs the tiny impurities, forming a larger mass that will then be trapped by filters. Lime is added to reach the desired pH, or acidity, of the water.

sterilization: The destruction of living microorganisms by using a substance, such as chlorine, or by heating.

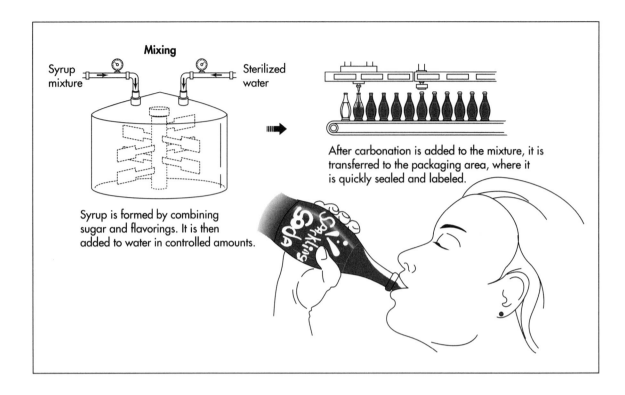

Mixing

Syrup mixture

Sterilized water

After carbonation is added to the mixture, it is transferred to the packaging area, where it is quickly sealed and labeled.

Syrup is formed by combining sugar and flavorings. It is then added to water in controlled amounts.

Filtering, sterilizing, and dechlorinating the water

2 The clarified water is poured through a sand filter to remove the particles of floc. First, the water passes through a layer of sand and then layers of fine and coarse gravel to trap the particles.

3 Bacteria and organic matter that might spoil the water's taste or color have to be destroyed. This is done by pumping the water into a storage tank in which a small amount of free chlorine is added. The chlorinated water is kept in the tank until the water is completely purified.

4 An activated carbon filter removes the chlorine and other remaining organic matter. (Activated carbon is carbon in the form of a powder or granules that purifies liquids by collecting impurities on its surface.) Then, a vacuum pump removes all the air from the water before it moves to a dosing station.

Mixing the ingredients

5 The dissolved sugar and flavors are pumped into a dosing station in a predetermined sequence. They are transported to batch tanks where they are carefully mixed to form a syrup. The syrup may be sterilized while in the tanks using ultraviolet radiation. Flash pasteurization may also be used to kill any microorganism in the syrup. This involves quickly heating and cooling the syrup. Fruit-based syrups generally must be pasteurized.

6 The water and syrup are carefully blended by proportioners, machines that control the amounts and flow rates of the two ingredients. To keep air from entering the mixture, carbon dioxide is used for pressure.

Carbonating the soft drink

7 Carbonation (the addition of carbon dioxide gas) is generally performed when the product is completed, although it may be done at an earlier stage. The temperature of the soft drink has to be controlled, so that it is not too cold, causing the carbon dioxide to dissolve in it when added.

The amount of carbon dioxide pressure added depends on the type of soft drink. For example, fruit drinks require less carbonation than mixer drinks, such as tonics, which are intended to be diluted with other liquids.

Filling and packaging

8 The finished beverage is poured into bottles or cans and immediately sealed with pressure-resistant closures. Closures used may be tinplate or steel crowns with corrugated (having parallel grooves and ridges) edges, twists-off caps, or pull-tabs.

9 Soft drinks are generally cooled during manufacture. Before labeling, the soft drinks are brought to room temperature to prevent condensation from ruining the labels. (Water vapor in the air will condense, or change to liquid, if it comes in contact with the cold containers.) This is done by spraying the containers with warm water and drying them. Labels, containing information about brand name, ingredients, shelf life, and safe use of the product, are then attached to the bottles. Most labels are made of paper, although some are made of plastic film. Cans are usually preprinted with product information before being filled.

10 Finally, the soft drinks are packed into cartons or trays, which are then loaded into pallets or crates to be shipped to distributors.

Quality Control

Soft drink manufacturers follow strict water quality standards for allowable dissolved solids, chlorides, sulfates, iron, and aluminum, as

The interior of a coin-operated soda machine. *Photograph by Kelly A. Quin. Copyright © Kelly A. Quin. Reproduced by permission of the photographer.*

well as water alkalinity. The use of clean water ensures that the finished products will have a consistent taste, flavor, and color. This means that a product sold in one area tastes and looks identical to the same product sold in another location. Effective removal of impure particles from the water facilitates the production process because blockage due to impurities is eliminated. Testing for the presence of microorganisms is done regularly.

The National Soft Drink Association and other agencies set standards for regulating the quality of all ingredients. Monitoring the quality of sugar is especially important. To prevent spoilage, sugar has to be carefully handled in dry, clean environments.

Raw materials are inspected as they arrive at the factory and before they are mixed with other ingredients because preservatives may not kill all bacteria. All tanks, machines, and containers are thoroughly sterilized. Cans that are made of aluminum alloy (a mixture of aluminum and another metal) or tin-coated low-carbon steel are lacquered (coated with a baked-on finish) internally to seal the metal and prevent corrosion when it comes in contact with the beverage.

THE FRANCHISE SYSTEM

Asa Candler (1851–1929), who bought the Coca-Cola recipe and brand name from its inventor, John Pemberton, developed the franchise system. Candler realized that water—the soft drink's main ingredient—being heavy, would be too costly to ship. Instead of bottling his product in Atlanta, Georgia, Candler granted franchises (authorization given by a manufacturer to a company or companies to sell his or her products in a certain area) to bottlers all over the country, authorizing them to mix the soft drink in their areas, adding carbonated water to his Coca-Cola syrup.

Manufacturers also recommend specific storage conditions to retailers to ensure that soft drinks do not spoil. The shelf life of soft drinks is about one year.

The Future

Nearly 450 different beverages are manufactured in the United States. Companies constantly develop new flavors. Most diet soft drinks use the sweetener aspartame, first approved for soft drinks in 1983 by the U.S. Food and Drug Administration (FDA). Manufacturers are always experimenting with new sweeteners that are several times sweeter than sugar. The sugar substitutes acesulfame-K and sucralose, approved for use in soft drinks in 1998, are used alone or combined with other sweeteners.

Trends in the soft drink industry continue to consider public health, safety, and the environment. New methods of water purification and sterilization will improve production and minimize the need for preservatives in soft drinks. On July 5, 2002, the FDA approved a new sugar substitute, neotame, for use in certain food products, including soft drinks. Depending on its use in food, neotame is 7,000 to 13,000 times sweeter than sugar.

For More Information

Books

Tchudi, Stephen N. *Soda Poppery: The History of Soft Drinks in America.* New York, NY: Charles Scribner's Sons, 1986.

Periodicals

Henkel, John. "Sugar Substitutes: Americans Opt for Sweetness and Lite." *FDA Consumer.* (November-December 1999): pp. 12–15.

"100 Years of Production Innovation." *Beverage World.* (January 1998): pp. 136–140.

Web Sites

"The Crown Cork Cap and Crown Soda Machine 1892 and 1898." *The American Society of Mechanical Engineers.* http://www.asme.org/history/brochures/h174.pdf (accessed on July 22, 2002).

Jacobson, Michael F. "Liquid Candy: How Soft Drinks Are Harming Americans' Health." *Center for Science in the Public Interest.* http://www.cspinet.org/sodapop/liquid_candy.htm (accessed on July 22, 2002).

"What's in Soft Drinks?" *National Soft Drink Association.* http://www.nsda.org/softdrinks/History/whatsin.html (accessed July 22, 2002).

Spacesuit

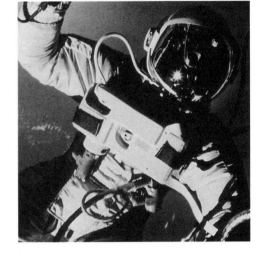

Reproduced by permission of AP/Wide World Photos.

A spacesuit is a pressurized (filled with air pressure) garment worn by astronauts during space flights. It is designed to protect them from potential dangerous conditions they may experience in space. A spacesuit is also called an Extravehicular Mobility Unit (EMU) because it is worn when an astronaut leaves the spacecraft in order to perform a variety of tasks, including the repair of satellites, collection of samples, taking of pictures, and assembling of equipment.

The spacesuit is designed to recreate the environmental conditions of Earth's atmosphere. It provides the basic necessities for life support, such as oxygen, temperature control, pressurized enclosure, carbon dioxide removal, and protection from sunlight, solar radiation, and micrometeoroids.

Each complete spacesuit costs over $12 million to make.

The white spacesuit weighs about 275 pounds (124.8 kilograms) on Earth. However, above Earth's atmosphere, or in space, it has no weight at all due to the near absence of gravity. Contrary to popular belief, it is not true that there is absolutely no gravity in space. What is commonly referred to as zero gravity in space is more accurately called microgravity, or very little gravity. Just the same, spacesuits are weightless in space.

The spacesuit is reusable and has a product life expectancy of about fifteen years. The suit is pressurized to 4.3 pounds per square inch (0.302 kilogram per square centimeter) and can be recharged by hooking up to the orbiter (piloted part of a spacecraft). Unlike previous spacesuits, which were tailor-made for each astronaut, today's spacesuits can be assembled from standard-sized parts to fit any body size. The basic interchangeable sections include the helmet, the hard upper torso, the arms, and the lower torso. These parts are adjustable and can be resized. Each complete spacesuit has fourteen layers and costs over $12 million to make.

Early spacesuits

The space age began in 1957 when the former Soviet Union launched *Sputnik,* an unmanned, artificial (manmade) satellite, into space. In 1958, the United States created the National Aeronautics and Space Administration (NASA) to develop space exploration. The first spacesuits were introduced around this time and have since undergone changes that resulted in a more functional, although more complicated, design.

Astronauts of the *Mercury* program, the first U.S.-manned space program, in the early 1960s wore a pressure suit patterned after those worn by U.S. Navy high-altitude jet aircraft pilots. On May 5, 1961, Alan B. Shepard Jr. (1923–1998), America's first man in space, wore such a suit, made of only two layers of nylon fabric with fabric breaks in the elbow and knee areas for movement.

The *Mercury* astronauts wore the spacesuits unpressurized, or uninflated. They could pressurize the suits in the event that the spacecraft cabin lost pressure, which never occurred in any of their six missions.

Next, designers developed a five-layer spacesuit. Like the first spacesuits, it could be pressurized when necessary. The layer closest to the body was a white cotton undergarment with attachments for biomedical devices, such as a heart-rate monitor. A blue nylon layer that provided comfort was next. The third layer consisted of a black, pressurized, neoprene-coated nylon that provided oxygen in the absence of cabin pressure. A Teflon® layer served to hold the suit's shape when pressurized. The final layer was a white nylon material that reflected sunlight and guarded against accidental damage.

Spacesuit for the *Gemini* spacewalkers

Of the twelve *Gemini* missions between 1964 and 1966, ten were manned launches. For these first spacewalks ever undertaken by astronauts, a seven-layer suit was designed. The extra layers were made up of aluminized Mylar®, which provided protection against extreme heat and micrometeoroids. Micrometeoroids are very tiny particles of matter left over from the formation of the solar system and from the collisions of comets and aster-

airlock: An airtight chamber between two places with differing air pressure, such as between the inside and the outside of a space capsule, and in which the air pressure can be changed to match that of either place.

astronaut: A person trained to pilot a spacecraft and/or perform scientific experiments in space.

biomedical: Having to do with the study of the human body's ability to survive under environmental stresses and conditions, such as while traveling in space.

capsule: A pressurized vehicle that transports astronauts on space flights.

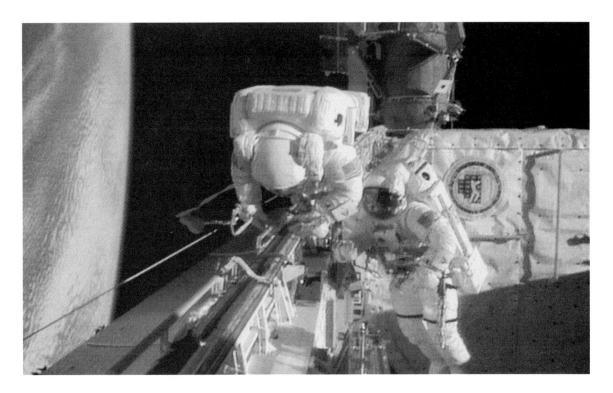

U.S. astronauts Rich Clifford and Linda Godwin wear full spacesuits during their spacewalk outside the space shuttle *Atlantis* and the Russian space station *Mir* on March 27, 1996. *Reproduced by permission of AP/Wide World Photos.*

oids. These particles travel at very high speeds and are capable of penetrating human skin. The spacesuit weighed 33 pounds (15 kilograms).

Suiting for moon walks

The *Apollo* Program, conducted between 1961 and 1972, was designed to land an astronaut on the moon and bring the person back to Earth. On July 20, 1969, Neil A. Armstrong (1930–) and Edwin E. "Buzz" Aldrin Jr. (1930–) became the first two persons to walk on the moon. Ten other *Apollo* astronauts walked on the moon after that.

For moon walks, the astronauts wore a seven-layer spacesuit with a life-support backpack. The total weight was about 57 pounds (26 kilograms). As with the *Mercury* and *Gemini* suits, the *Apollo* garment had to function as a pressure suit in the event of cabin pressure loss. The spacesuit was constructed so that it not only allowed movement of the shoulders and arms but also of the legs. The astronauts had to be able to bend and stoop down so that they could collect samples on the moon to take

micrometeoroids: Very tiny particles of matter left over from the formation of the solar system and from the collisions of comets and asteroids that travel at very high speeds in space and are capable of penetrating human skin.

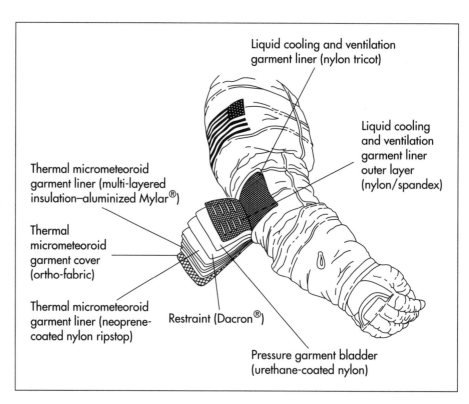

Liquid cooling and ventilation garment liner (nylon tricot)

Liquid cooling and ventilation garment liner outer layer (nylon/spandex)

Thermal micrometeoroid garment liner (multi-layered insulation–aluminized Mylar®)

Thermal micrometeoroid garment cover (ortho-fabric)

Thermal micrometeoroid garment liner (neoprene-coated nylon ripstop)

Restraint (Dacron®)

Pressure garment bladder (urethane-coated nylon)

A variety of fabric materials are used to make a modern EMU.

neoprene: A synthetic, or artificial, rubber that is resistant to heat, light, and most solvents.

orbiter: The piloted section of a spacecraft that travels through space and lands like an airplane.

pressurize: To maintain normal air pressure in the enclosed environment of a spacesuit or a spacecraft.

satellite: A manmade object that orbits Earth, such as a communications satellite used to transmit television programs.

space shuttle: A reusable spacecraft consisting of an orbiter, two solid rocket boosters, and an external fuel tank; used to carry out a variety of missions, including deploying satellites into space and conducting science experiments.

back to Earth. The design of the suit also had to take into consideration the extreme heat of the lunar day and the micrometeoroids that slammed against the lunar surface.

Raw Materials

A spacesuit is made from numerous raw materials. Fabric materials include a variety of synthetic polyester. The innermost layer is made of nylon tricot. The second layer is made of spandex, a synthetic stretch fabric. The pressure garment is made of urethane-coated nylon. On top of this is Dacron®, a type of polyester that acts as a restraint and keeps the pressure garment from ballooning. Other synthetic fabrics include neoprene, aluminized Mylar®, Gortex®, Kevlar®, and Nomex®. Many of these synthetic fabrics have been known for their outstanding properties. For example, Kevlar® has been used for making bulletproof vests for the police for more than two decades, and Nomex®, with its heat- and flame-resistant properties, is the fabric used by firefighters and race car drivers.

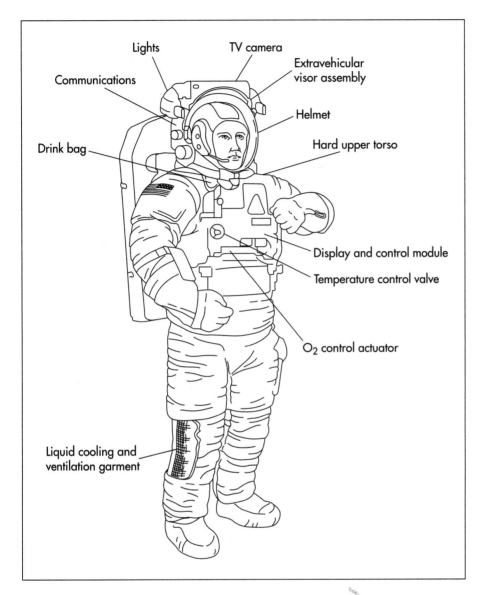

Lights

TV camera

Extravehicular
visor assembly

Communications

Helmet

Drink bag

Hard upper torso

Display and control module

Temperature control valve

O_2 control actuator

Liquid cooling and
ventilation garment

An Extravehicular Mobility Unit (EMU).

Aside from the fabric materials, other raw materials play important roles. Fiberglass (made from compressed glass fibers) is the primary material for the hard upper torso. Lithium hydroxide and activated charcoal make up the filter that removes carbon dioxide and water vapor during a spacewalk. A silver zinc blend makes up the battery that powers the suit. Plastic tubing is woven into the fabric to transport cooling water

spacewalk: A short trip by an astronaut outside the spacecraft to perform a task.

throughout the suit. A polycarbonate (plastic) material is used to build the helmet shell. Different components are used to make up the electric circuitry and suit controls.

Design

A spacesuit or Extravehicular Mobility Unit (EMU) is constructed from various tailor-made components manufactured by more than eighty companies. EMUs come in standard-sized parts that are assembled by NASA.

The primary-life support system is a self-contained backpack with an oxygen supply, carbon-dioxide removal filters, caution and warning system, electrical power, water-cooling equipment, ventilating fan, machinery, and radio. The suit tank contains enough oxygen to last for seven hours. A secondary oxygen pack in the spacesuit provides emergency oxygen to last another thirty minutes.

The helmet is a large, plastic, pressure bubble with a neck-disconnect ring and a ventilation-distribution pad. It has a backup purge valve, which is used with the secondary oxygen pack to remove exhaled carbon dioxide. Also in the helmet is a tube that extends from a drink bag in the hard upper torso. The tube acts like a straw for drinking the water in the drink bag.

The helmet has an extravehicular visor assembly (EVA) with a sun-filtering visor, a clear impact-protective visor, and adjustable blinders. A light-bar attachment sits on top of the EVA. It consists of small flood lamps that light up areas not reached by sunlight or other sources of light. Also mounted on the EVA is a television camera system through which the crew inside the orbiter and mission controllers on Earth can see what the astronaut sees in space. It also enables those personnel to offer advice when needed.

The communications carrier assembly (CCA), also called a "Snoopy cap," is a fabric cap fitted with earphones and a microphone. It is attached to the spacesuit electrical harness and worn on the head.

A liquid cooling and ventilation garment comes next. It looks like a pair of longjohns with a zippered front and is made of stretchable spandex. It is fitted with about 300 feet (91.5 meters) of plastic cooling tubes through which chilled water is circulated. Since spacesuits trap heat, the circulating water keeps the astronaut cool. The astronaut can stop the circulation if he or she gets too cold.

The lower torso, which is put on before the hard upper torso, is made up of the pants, a maximum absorption garment (adult-size diaper), boots, the lower half of the waist closure, and knee and ankle joints. The pants consist of a pressure garment bladder (an inflatable garment) made of urethane-coated nylon, followed by a Dacron® restraint layer to keep the bladder from ballooning. Seven layers of aluminized Mylar® materials provide insulation, followed by the outer layer made of fabric blends of Gortex®, Kevlar®, and Nomex® materials. The lower torso can be made shorter or

Eileen Collins, the first woman pilot of a U.S. space shuttle, is shown without her spacesuit on. *Reproduced by permission of AP/Wide World Photos.*

longer by adjusting the sizing rings in the thigh and leg section. The boots have an insulated toe cap to improve heat retention. Thermal socks are also worn.

The arm assembly is adjustable just like the lower torso. It has a glove-attaching closure. The gloves contain miniature battery-powered heaters in each finger. The rest of the unit is covered by padding and an additional protective outer layer. The gloves have loops for attaching tethers (a ropelike restraint) for holding small tools and equipment.

An important component of the upper half of the suit is the hard upper torso, which is made of a fiberglass shell under fabric layers of the thermal micrometeoroid garment. It resembles the breast and back plates of a suit of armor. The hard upper torso is a mounting structure for different components, including the helmet, arms, lower torso, the upper half of the waste closure, the electrical harness, and the drink bag. In addition,

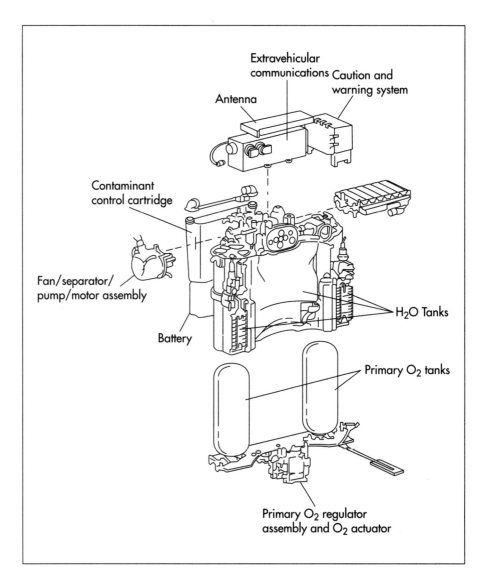

The primary life-support system is a self-contained backpack fitted with an oxygen supply, carbon-dioxide removal filters, electrical power, ventilating fan, and communications equipment.

the primary life-support system attaches at the back, while the display and control module that runs it attaches on the front.

The chest-mounted display and control module contains a digital display panel and all electrical and mechanical operating controls. It enables the astronaut to connect to external sources of fluids and electricity. The module is connected to the warning system in the upper torso to let the astronaut know the status of the suit's environment. A purge valve in the module can be opened, allowing contaminated gases and water vapor to flow out of the valve into space.

When the upper torso is not in use, it is connected to the orbiter air-lock (airtight chamber) support system through a service and cooling umbilical line. Connections within the umbilical line allow the orbiter to provide the spacesuit with electrical power, cooling water, and oxygen, so that the contents of the primary life-support system are conserved. The umbilical line is also used for battery recharging. A silver zinc recharge-able battery, operating at seventeen volts, powers the suit.

The Manufacturing Process

The manufacture of a modern spacesuit consists of two phases. First, the individual components are constructed. Then, the finished components are brought to a primary manufacture location, such as the NASA headquarters in Houston, Texas, and put together.

Helmet and visor assembly

1 The helmet and visor are constructed using injection molding. Pellets of polycarbonate, or plastic, are melted and then forced under high pressure into a mold with the shape of the helmet/visor. As it cools, the plastic assumes the shape of the mold. A connecting device is added to the open end of the helmet so that it can be attached to the hard upper torso. The ventilation distribution pad and the purge valves are added before the helmet is packaged and shipped. The visor assembly is fitted with a "head lamp" and communications equipment.

Primary life-support systems

2 The primary life-support system has several components, which are put together one at a time. Then all the pieces are put into the backpack unit. First, the pressurized oxygen tanks are filled, capped, and put into the backpack. The carbon-dioxide removal equipment is assembled. This consists of a filter canister filled with lithium hydroxide and activated charcoal, which is attached to a hose. The backpack is then fitted with a ventilating fan system, a radio, a warning system, and the water-cooling equipment. When completed, the life-support system is attached to the hard upper torso.

Display and control module

3 The key components of the display and control module are built as separate units and then assembled. This allows the parts to be easily serviced if necessary. The module contains all the electronic and mechanical operating controls, a digital display, and other electronic interfaces. The purge valve is also added to the module.

Liquid cooling and ventilation garment

4 The liquid cooling and ventilation garment makes up the first two layers of the spacesuit that are worn next the skin. Nylon tricot is first cut into a garment that resembles a pair of longjohns. Meanwhile, the spandex fibers are woven into a sheet of fabric and cut into the same shape. The spandex is fitted with a series of plastic cooling tubes 300 feet (91.5 meters) long and sewn to the nylon material. A front zipper is attached, as well as connectors for attachments to the life-support system.

Upper and lower torso

5 The various layers of synthetic fibers for the pants, arm assembly, and gloves are woven together and then cut into the appropriate shapes. The segments are then attached. Waist closures are added for attaching to the upper torso. The arm assembly is fitted with glove-attaching closures. The gloves are fitted with miniature heaters in every finger, then covered with padding and a protective outer layer.

6 The hard upper torso is made from fiberglass and metal. It has four openings where the lower torso, arms, and helmet attach. Adapters are added on the front and back for attachment of the primary life-support system and the display and control module.

Final assembly

7 The finished components are shipped to NASA for assembly. This is done on the ground so that the spacesuit can be tested before being used in space.

Quality Control

The individual suppliers conduct quality tests at each step of the manufacturing process. The manufacturers make sure they satisfy NASA standards, ensuring that the suits will function in the extreme environment of space. They check for such things as air leakage, depressurization, and

"BENDS" PREVENTION

Before astronauts can venture out to space, they have to prebreathe pure oxygen. This is done to prevent decompression sickness called the "bends." Decompression sickness results from exposure to low atmospheric pressure, which causes the nitrogen in the blood to evaporate, forming bubbles in the blood. These bubbles interfere with blood flow, causing joint pains, cramps, paralysis, and even death. Nitrogen bubble formation will occur if the astronaut steps into the very-low-pressure environment (4.3 pounds per square inch, or 0.302 kilogram per square centimeter) of the spacesuit from the higher-pressure setting of the space cabin (the same pressure as the earth's atmosphere; 14.7 pounds per square inch, or 1.034 kilograms per square centimeter). To replace the nitrogen in the blood, before putting on their spacesuits, astronauts prebreathe oxygen through an oxygen mask attached to an oxygen supply. After their suits are on and before the pressure in the suits is lowered, the astronauts prebreathe more oxygen.

defective life-support systems. The testings are very important because even a single malfunction could have serious adverse results for an astronaut in space.

The Future

The EMU design used today is a product of many years of research and development. However, research continues to perfect this design. One area that can be improved is a suit that would provide more pressure so that the "prebreathing" time can be reduced. (See sidebar.) Resizing of the suit in orbit also needs more research. Currently, it takes a significant amount of time to remove or add extending inserts in the leg and arm areas. The electronic controls of the suit also need improvement. Researchers are working on replacing the complex command codes with buttons that just have to be pressed.

For More Information

Books

Dyson, Marianne J. *Space Station Science: Life in Free Fall.* New York, NY: Scholastic, Inc., 1999.

Richie, Jason. *Spectacular Space Travelers.* Minneapolis, MN: The Oliver Press, Inc., 2001.

Vogt, Gregory L. *Suited for Spacewalking*. Washington, DC: National Aeronautics and Space Administration, 1998.

Periodicals

Lucid, Shannon W. "Six Months on Mir." *Scientific American*. (May 1998): pp. 46-55.

Samuel, Eugenie. "Super Skin." *New Scientist*. (June 16, 2001): p. 24.

Web Sites

"International Space Station: Turning Science Fiction into Science Fact."

National Aeronautics and Space Administration. http://www.hq.nasa.gov/office/pao/facts/HTML/FS-004-HQ.html (accessed July 22, 2002).

Portree, David S.F. and Robert C. Treviño. *Walking to Olympus: An EVA Chronology*. http://spaceflight.nasa.gov/spacenews/factsheets/pdfs/EVACron.pdf (accessed on July 22, 2002).

"Women's Achievements in Aviation and Space." *National Aeronautics and Space Administration*. http://www.nasa.gov/hqpao/women_ac.htm (accessed on July 22, 2002).

Television

Photograph by Kelly A. Quin. Copyright © Kelly A. Quin. Reproduced by permission of the photographer.

The device known as the television is actually a receiver that is the end point of a system that transmits pictures and sounds at a distance. The process starts with a television camera that converts all image information into electrical signals, which are delivered to homes and businesses through a television antenna, underground fiber optic cable, or satellite. The function of the receiver, or television set, is to unscramble the electrical signals, converting them into sounds and pictures.

Television is one of the greatest technological developments of all time. It did not happen overnight, but developed over a number of years, taking advantage of advances in the sciences and technologies of the time. Television has not only been a source of entertainment worldwide, but it has also linked people through their common experience of witnessing events that are happening in different parts of the world and beyond. For example, on July 20, 1969, about 720 million people all over the world watched on television as astronaut Neil Armstrong walked on the moon.

In the United States, about 99 percent of households own at least one television set, and over 60 percent subscribe to cable television.

In the United States, about 99 percent of households own at least one television set. Over 60 percent subscribe to cable television. The average household watches approximately seven hours of television each day.

A group effort

No single person invented the television. Instead, it is the result of scientific research in various countries over several decades. In 1817, Baron

Jöns Jakob Berzelius (1779–1848), a Swedish chemist, identified selenium as a chemical element. He found that selenium could conduct electricity and that this ability to conduct electricity varied with the amount of light hitting it. In 1878, Sir William Crookes (1832–1919), a British chemist and physicist, first mentioned cathode rays (beams of electrons in a glass vacuum tube). These scientific findings occurred separately and would take many years to be applied to the making of television.

In 1884, German engineer Paul Nipkow (1860–1940) built the first crude television with the help of a mechanical scanning disk. Small holes on the rotating disk picked up pieces of images and imprinted them on a light-sensitive selenium tube. A receiver then recreated the image pieces into a whole picture. Nipkow's mechanical invention, crude as it was, employed the scanning principle that would be used by future television cameras and receivers to record and recreate images for a television screen.

Television goes electronic

In 1911, while some scientists were trying to improve on Nipkow's mechanical scanning disk, Scottish electrical engineer Alan Archibald Campbell Swinton (1863–1930) discussed his idea of a "distant electric vision," using cathode rays. Although Swinton never built the electronic television that he so accurately described, other scientists brought into reality his idea of the television set as we know it today.

In 1897, German scientist Ferdinand Karl Braun (1850–1918) invented the cathode ray tube. Inside the glass tube, cathode rays could produce pictures by hitting the fluorescent (glowing) screen at the end of the tube. Boris Rosing of Russia demonstrated in 1907 that the cathode ray tube could serve as the receiver of a television system.

In England, John Logie Baird (1888–1946) experimented with Nipkow's scanning disk in the early 1920s. At around the same time, in the United States, Charles Francis Jenkins (1867–1934) was performing the same experiment. In 1926, Baird was the first to demonstrate the electrical transmission of images in motion.

The invention of television cameras during the 1920s further contributed to the development of television. Philo Farnsworth (1906–1971) of Idaho was only fifteen years old when he figured out the workings of an electronic television system. Farnsworth invented the image dissector tube, an electronic scanner. In 1927, he gave the first public demonstration of the electronic television by transmitting the image of a dollar sign. Along with another American, Allen B. Dumont (1901–1965), Farnsworth

antenna: A device used in television to send and receive electromagnetic waves, or waves of electrical and magnetic force brought about by the vibration of electrons.

cable television: The transmission of television programs from television stations to home television sets through fiber optic cable or metal cable.

cathode ray tube (CRT): A vacuum tube whose front part makes up the television screen. In the tube, images are formed by electrons striking the phosphor-coated screen.

developed a pickup tube that became the home television set by 1939.

At the same time, Russian immigrant Vladimir Zworykin (1889–1982) invented an electronic camera tube called the iconoscope. Both television cameras invented by Farnsworth and Zworykin used a cathode ray tube as the television receiver for recreating the original images.

Color television

The earliest mention of color television was in a German patent in the early 1900s.

In 1928, John Logie Baird used Nipkow's mechanical scanning disk to demonstrate color television. A color television system developed by Hungarian-born American Peter Goldmark (1906–1977) in 1940 did not receive wide acceptance because it did not work in black-and-white television sets. It took almost twenty years for color television to be commercially available.

Inventor and television pioneer Philo T. Farnsworth shows early television components. *Reproduced by permission of Corbis Corporation.*

Raw Materials

The television is made up of four principal sets of parts: the exterior part or housing, the picture tube, the audio (sound) reception and stereo system, and the electronic components (parts). These electronics parts include cable and antenna input and output devices, a built-in antenna in most television sets, a remote control receiver, computer chips, and access buttons. The remote control, popularly called a "clicker," is an additional part of the television set.

The television housing is made of injection-molded plastic. In injection molding, liquid plastic is forced into a mold with the help of high pressure. The plastic takes on the shape of the mold as it cools. Some television sets may have exterior wooden cabinets. The audio reception and stereo systems are made of metal and plastic.

The picture tube materials consist of glass and a coating made of the chemical phosphor, which glows when hit by light. Other picture tube materials include electronic attachments around and at the rear of the tube. Brackets and braces hold the picture tube inside the housing.

The antenna and most of the input-output connections are made of metal. Some of the input-output connections are coated with plastic or

chip: Also called microchip, a very small piece of silicon that carries interconnected electronic components.

electron: A small particle within an atom that carries a negative charge, which is the basic charge of electricity.

fiber optic cable: A bundle of hair-thin glass fibers that carry information as beams of light.

Television uses a process called scanning to capture and then recreate an image. When recording an image, the television camera breaks it down into 525 horizontal lines. Electron beams in the camera tube scan (read) the lines thirty times every second. (In Europe, Australia, and most countries in Asia, each image is separated into 625 lines, with the scanning done at twenty-five times per second.) The television receiver, which is the television set, recreates the images on the screen by using the same electrical signals recorded by the television camera. The picture tube inside the television contains three electron guns that receive the video (image) signals. The electron guns shoot electron beams at the phosphor-coated dots on the screen, scanning the screen in the same pattern that the images were recorded by the camera.

special metals to improve the quality of the connection or to insulate it. (The insulation material prevents the escape of heat, electricity, or sound.) The chips (also called microchips) are made of silicon, metal, and solder (a metal that is heated and used to join metals).

Design

Different types of engineers are responsible for designing a television set. These include electronics, audio, video, plastics, and fiber optics engineers. The engineering team may design a bigger television set patterned after an existing model. They may also design new features, including an improved picture, better sound system, or a remote control that can work with other devices, such as a DVD player.

The team members discuss ideas about the new features, redrawing plans as they develop new ideas about the design. After the engineers receive initial approval for manufacturing the set, they make a prototype, or a model, after which the other sets will be patterned. A prototype is important for testing out the design, appearance, and functions of the set. Having a prototype also enables the production engineers to determine the production processes, machining (the cutting, shaping, and finishing by machine), tools, robots, and changes to existing factory production lines.

When the prototype passes a series of strict tests and is finally approved for manufacture by management, the engineers draw detailed plans and produce specifications for the design and production of the model. Specifications include the type of materials needed, their sizes, and workmanship involved in the manufacturing process.

fluorescent: Giving off light when exposed to electric current.

Raw materials and components that are manufactured by other persons are ordered. The production line is constructed and tested. Finally, the components that would go into the new television sets are put together in the assembly line.

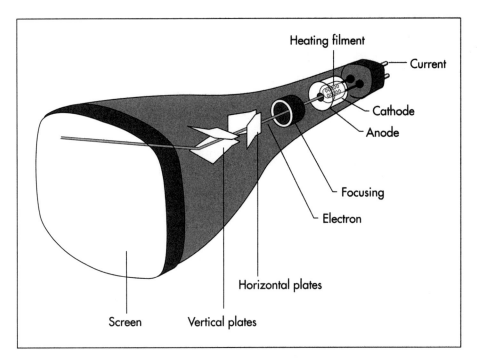

Heating filment
Current
Cathode
Anode
Focusing
Electron
Horizontal plates
Screen   Vertical plates

The Manufacturing Process

Housing

1 Television housings are mostly made of plastic. Using a process called injection molding, high pressure is applied to liquid plastic to force it into molds. The plastic is allowed to cool and harden. The formed solid plastics are released from the molds, trimmed, and cleaned. They are then assembled to make up the television housing. The molds are designed so that brackets and supports for the various parts of the television set are part of the housing.

Picture tube

2 The television picture tube, also called a cathode ray tube (CRT), is shaped like a funnel. The widest part of the funnel is a slightly curved plate made of glass. The glass is the television screen on which pictures are viewed. A dark tint may be added to the glass plate to improve color. The inside of the screen is covered with tiny dots of phosphors, or chemicals that glow when hit by electrons. The phosphor dots come in the primary colors red, green, and blue.

persistence of vision: A physical phenomenon in which the retina of the eye holds on to an image for a fraction of a second longer after it has seen the image. The brain, which works with the eye, puts these still images together so that the eye perceives them as a single movement.

phosphor: A chemical that glows when struck by light.

satellite: An object that is put into space and used to receive and send television signals over long distances.

scan: To move electrons over a surface in order to transmit an image.

3 Immediately behind the phosphor layer is a thin metal shadow mask with thousands of small holes. Some shadow masks are made of iron. The better-quality shadow masks are made of a mixture of nickel and iron called Invar that lets the picture tube operate at a higher temperature. Higher temperatures result in brighter pictures.

4 The narrow end of the color picture tube contains three electron guns. Their job is to shoot electron beams at the phosphors, with each gun responsible for a specific color. The shadow mask makes sure the electron guns each shoot at one color of phosphors in a process called scanning (see sidebar on page 272). When hit by electrons, the phosphors light up, creating the pictures on the television screen.

After the electron guns are placed inside the picture tube, air is removed from the tube to prevent it from interfering with the movement of the electrons. Then, the end of the tube is closed off with a fitted electrical plug that will be placed near the back of the set.

5 A deflection yoke, consisting of two electromagnetic coils, is fitted around the neck of the picture tube. The electromagnetic coils cause pulses of high voltage to guide the direction and speed of the electron beams as they scan the television screen.

Audio system

6 The speakers, which go into the housing, are typically made by another company that works closely with the television manufacturer. They are made according to certain characteristics specified by the manufacturer. Wiring, electronic sound controls, and integrated circuitry are assembled in the television set as it travels along the assembly line. An integrated circuit, also called a chip or microchip, is a tiny piece of silicon on which electronic parts and their interconnections are imprinted.

Electronic parts

7 After the picture tube and the audio system are assembled in the set, other electronic parts are added to the rear of the set. The antenna, cable jacks, other input and output jacks, and the electronics for receiving remote control signals are prepared as subassemblies on anoth-

er assembly line or by specialty contractors hired from outside the company. These electronic components are added to the set, and the housing is closed.

Quality Control

Like other precision products, the television requires strict quality control during manufacture. Inspections, laboratory testing, and field testing are constantly conducted during the development of prototypes. The manufacturer has to be sure the resulting product is not only technologically sound but also safe for use in homes and businesses.

The Future

Researchers continue to find new ways to improve on television sets. The high-definition television (HDTV) system that we have today is a digital television system. The conventional television system

A flat-panel television. *Reproduced by permission of AP/Wide World Photos.*

transmits signals using radio waves. During transmission, these waves could get distorted, for example, by bad weather. The television set, unable to distinguish between distorted and good-quality waves, converts all the radio waves it receives into pictures. Therefore, the resulting images may not all be of good quality.

Digital television, on the other hand, while also using radio waves, assigns a code to the radio waves. When it comes time to recreate the picture, the television set obtains information from the code on how to display the image. HDTV offers clearer and sharper images with its 1,125-line picture. Compared to the traditional 525-line picture, HDTV offers a far better picture because more lines are scanned by the television camera and receiver. This means more details of the images are included.

In the future, digital television could also allow the viewer to choose camera angles while watching a concert or a sports event. The viewer

silicon: A nonmetallic material widely used in microchips because of its ability to conduct electricity.

could also communicate with the host of a live program and edit movies on screen.

Flat-panel television screens, such as liquid-crystal display (LCD) and plasma screens, are being perfected to achieve the kind of picture and sound seen in movie theaters. They are also seen as replacements for the present bulky television sets made of cathode ray tubes. The flat screens are not only lightweight but are also energy-efficient. However, unless these state-of-the art technologies become affordable, it will be a while before consumers convert to flat-screen televisions.

For More Information

Books

Graham, Ian. *Communications*. Austin, TX: Steck-Vaughn Company, 2001.

Graham, Ian. *Radio and Television*. Austin, TX: Steck-Vaughn Company, 2001.

Parker, Steve, Peter Lafferty, and Steve Setford. *How Things Work*. New York, NY: Barnes & Noble Books, 2001.

Periodicals

Brown-Kenyon, Paul I., Alan Miles, and John S. Rose,. "Unscrambling Digital TV." *McKinsey Quarterly*. (2000): pp.71-81.

Kubey, Robert, and Mihaly Csikszentmihalyi. "Television Addiction." *Scientific American*. (February 2000).

Web Sites

Early Television Foundation. http://www.earlytelevision.org (accessed on July 22, 2002).

"The Revolution of Television." *Technical Press*. http://www.tvhandbook.com/History/History_TV.htm (accessed on July 22, 2002).

Video Game

Reproduced by permission of AP/Wide World Photos.

A video game is an electronic or computerized game played by making images move on a television screen, computer monitor, or coin-operated arcade. Some video games are played on hand-held, battery-powered devices. Even though many homes have personal computers, consoles (home video game systems) are as popular as ever, and manufacturers continue to create new models. Consoles are computers made just for playing video games, are easy to hook up to the television set, and typically allow for multiple players.

The video game industry is on a roll. An estimated 60 percent of Americans play video games regularly. Among teenagers aged eight to eleven, over 80 percent play video games. In 2001, the video game industry made $9.4 billion in sales.

About 250,000 individual commands are written by programmers to create a video game program.

World's first video game

The world's first video game was created by a group of MIT (Massachusetts Institute of Technology) computer programmers and scientists during the early 1960s. Led by Steve Russell, the group did not set out to design an electronic game. They simply wanted to test a new computer. Russell wrote a computer program for a two-player game he called *Spacewar*. The game featured battling spaceships that fired torpedoes. Although the game became popular among other computer programmers and the people with whom they shared it, it did not give birth to the video game industry.

A quarter a game

In 1971, influenced by Steve Russell's *Spacewar,* Nolan Bushnell (1943–) invented *Computer Space,* the first coin-operated arcade game. Bushnell also built a small machine just for the game. However, his game was so complicated that people lost interest in it.

In 1972, Bushnell and his partner, Ted Dabney, introduced an arcade game called *Pong.* Designed by Alan Alcorn, it was modeled after the game of Ping-Pong™, or table tennis. For a quarter a game, players tried to hit a flashing dot (the "ball") past their opponent's video paddles. Based on the phenomenal success of the arcade video game, Bushnell and Dabney started the Atari Company in 1975, introducing a home version of *Pong.* A *Pong* console, or home video game system, that attached to the television set was developed for home play. Giving Sears, Roebuck, and Company the exclusive right to sell the game, Atari sold 150,000 units of the *Home Pong* console and game. In 1975, Bushnell sold the company to Warner Communications for $28 million.

Dots on a television screen

burn: To write the digital information into the light-sensitive metal layer of a compact disk.

console: A home video game system.

converted graphics: Images that are drawn using a computer program.

digitized image: Image that has been converted into digital codes, or number codes, that computers can read.

While Bushnell and Dabney were developing *Pong,* Ralph Baer (1922–) was designing a home video game system. In 1972, Magnavox introduced Baer's invention, the Odyssey. The Odyssey came with six program cards for playing twelve different games, including tennis, football, hockey, and skiing. The game, played on the television screen, consisted of three white dots, two of which served as paddles for hitting the third dot back and forth. Plastic overlays, which players placed over the television screen, provided the playing fields. For example, a plastic overlay of a hockey rink came with the hockey game. Nearly 100,000 systems were sold that first year.

Success and collapse

Rapid advances in electronics technology during the 1970s led to the development of more complicated games. In 1978, Atari's *Football* and Midway's *Space Invaders* became the all-time favorites in arcades up to that point. *Pac-Man,* produced by Midway and Japan's Namco, became

Two boys play a video hockey game on a television. *Reproduced by permission of Corbis Corporation.*

the 1980 superstar, with about 300,000 units sold worldwide. Ten sequels were created following the initial *Pac-Man* craze.

Companies flooded the market with home video game systems and rushed to adapt popular arcade games to video cartridges. Consumers were overwhelmed with the large number of games, many of which were of poor quality but were still expensive. By 1983, the home video game business had started to collapse. The 1983 sales of $3 billion had dropped to $100 million by 1985. Interestingly, arcade video games continued to flourish.

Bigger and better

In 1986, the Japanese company Nintendo rekindled Americans' interest in video games with such games as the *Super Mario Bros.* and the *Legend of Zelda.* Whereas previous home video games were poor imitations of arcade games, Nintendo's games were genuine reproductions of their arcade counterparts. In 1989, Nintendo introduced a handheld video game system called Game Boy, which came with *Tetris,* a puzzle block

electroforming: The process of making a copy of the master compact disk by using an electric current to apply a nickel coating onto the surface of the disk and then separating the metal coating from the master disk.

frame: A single strip of film, several of which are put together to show an action.

game designed by Russian Alexi Pajitnov that remains popular to this day. That same year, Sega, also a Japanese company, released the Genesis home video game system. Its *Sonic the Hedgehog* game became a favorite game in 1991, followed by a sequel, which was an instant hit.

In the late 1990s, video games took advantage of new technologies, such as the compact disks (CDs) and digital video disks (DVDs). Computer games were created when personal computers became available to more people in the mid-1980s. Today, video games are not just toys. They have become a part of the computer and Internet technology.

Design

A team of people, consisting of computer programmers, writers, artists, musicians, and other game designers, are responsible for the design of a video game. During the design process, they work out details of the game, including the game type, objective, and graphics (pictures).

The team decides the type of game, which may be one of six categories. These include fighting, shooting, strategy, simulations, adventure, and RJA (run, jump, and avoid) games. Fighting games require the players to battle with each other or with the computer. They are generally the most popular games and include such titles as *Street Fighter* and *Mortal Kombat*. In shooting games, the player tries to destroy enemy tanks, ships, or planes. Strategy games include chess, checkers, or bridge. Simulation games reproduce real-world activities, such as driving a race car or flying a plane, while adventure games let the players do role-playing, such as being a wizard or a warrior. The RJA games, such as the *Super Mario Bros.* games, let a player reach a goal while having to overcome various obstacles.

Raw Materials

A vivid imagination is the most important raw material in creating a video game. However, a variety of supplies are needed to produce and market the designer's ideas.

The Manufacturing Process

Designing and producing a video game involves the efforts of many people. Creating the computer program and images alone requires at least twenty people. The development of the game can be a long, drawn-out process that can sometimes take up to one year.

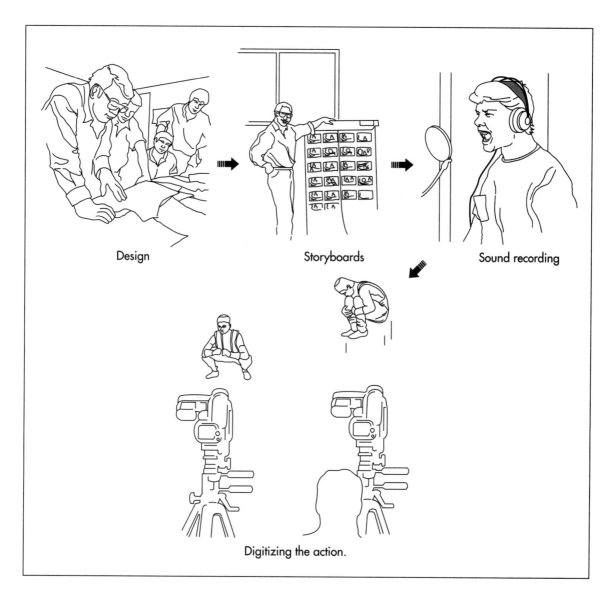

Design

Storyboards

Sound recording

Digitizing the action.

Creating a video game is a long, multifaceted process. A team of designers, artists, actors, and computer programmers work together to create the final product.

Creating the story

1 The first step in video game manufacture is writing the game's story, complete with a setting, characters, and plot. This provides an objective for the player and a guideline for the rules of the game. A game manual is usually produced, using all this information.

The designer may also be the writer of the story. Or, other writers may help create the story. The writers make storyboards, which are a series of one-panel sketches pinned on a baseboard. The sketches outline the scenes, which are arranged in their order of occurrence. Dialogue and/or summaries of action are written under each sketch.

Capturing action with art

2 After the story is outlined and the type of game is agreed upon, the team decides on the game's format. The format is the way the video game is presented to the player. The formats include platform, top-down, scrolling, isometric, three-dimensional (3-D), and text.

The platform format features a side view of the player's character. The top-down format gives a bird's-eye view of the player's character and is the format often used for war games. Scrolling involves moving the screen slowly in one direction. The isometric format is a top-down game, which uses perspective tricks to give the illusion of 3D. The text format has limited graphics and is used only for interactive fiction. Video games may use one or more of these formats.

3 The artists add drawings to the storyboards. They also add character descriptions and arrows showing how the characters will move.

4 The artists create final pictures, using one of two methods. They may create converted graphics, which are images that have been drawn using a computer program. They may also make more lifelike images by filming the action with an actor and then electronically digitizing the images, or converting the images into the number codes of computers.

The artists review the taped actions on a color monitor and select each frame (a strip of film) that will be used to create a portion of an action. For example, six to ten frames are used to show a character taking one step. Four to five frames are needed to show a punch or a kick. The artists also create the background, using both converted graphics and digitized images.

Recording dialogue and sound effects

5 Dialogue and sound effects are recorded in a sound studio using various audio (sound) techniques. The sounds are recorded on digital audio tape and then computerized by a synthesizer. A synthesizer is a computer that translates sounds into computer data.

Computer chip board

After the game's program has been written and the recorded sound and action have been digitized, the game code is transferred to a master disk. This disk will be used to mass-produce thousands of copies of the game.

Writing the program

6 A team of programmers takes the design elements and starts writing the programs that will instruct the video game system or the computer on which the game will be played. The first step is to draw a flowchart, showing the logical steps of the computer program. Programming languages used include Visual Basic, Visual C++, Pascal, and Delphi. Each programmer in the team works on a different phase of the game, which can take up to seven months to produce.

To work more efficiently, the programmers use previously developed sequences of programming steps, adapting them to the new game. This saves additional time and efforts in rewriting the same programs and also helps reduce errors. Since computers perform their tasks by following the program instructions, any instruction error means that the video game would not function well. About 250,000 individual commands are written to create a video game program. Sounds and graphics are programmed separately.

Testing

7 The testing process helps reveal fundamental design and programming problems. It may be discovered that some elements of the design do not work very well or that certain parts may be too difficult

for the player. Programming problems may involve some illogical steps that the computer cannot follow.

Testing can be done in several ways. The programmers can play the game and try to find possible problems. Professional game testers, who are trained to look for errors that are not easily detected, may also be used. These people are typically game designers who have experience with many types of games. The game testers may suggest ways to make the game more entertaining or more challenging. The game developers may also invite consumers to test the game. This is an effective way to test the market. The suggestions and other information obtained are reviewed. Then, reprogramming is done until the desired results are achieved.

Burning the disks

8 When the programming is completed, the game code is transferred to a master compact disk (master CD). This process is called "burning" the CD. Creating a master disk is the first step in mass-producing copies of the game. The master disk is made of a smoothly polished glass coated with an adhesive and a layer of light-sensitive metal, such as aluminum. The disk is put in a laser-cutting machine. While the disk spins, the computer code from the game's program sends an electrical signal to the laser. A laser beam cuts grooves into the light-sensitive coating, recording the program information on the disk. The disk is soaked in a chemical that etches (eats away) the surfaces exposed to the laser beam, producing the pits and lands that carry the digital information. The disk is given a metal coating, usually silver.

9 Next, a metal negative copy of the master disk is made through a process called electroforming. Using an electric current, layers of nickel are applied onto the disk's surface. After the desired thickness is achieved, the nickel layer is separated from the master disk. This metal negative is an exact copy, but in reverse, of the master disk. (This is the first metal negative.) Using the same electroforming process, the metal negative is used to make several metal positives, or exact copies of the original master disk.

10 A mold called a stamper is made from a metal positive. This stamper, which is a metal negative (the second metal negative), is used to create the actual compact disk (CD) using a

Sony Computer Entertainment's executive vice president and chief operating officer, Kazuo Hirai, stands next to a display of PlayStations. Hirai was the creator of the popular video game. *Reproduced by permission of AP/Wide World Photos.*

process called injection molding. The stamper is placed into a mold in an injection molding machine. Melted polycarbonate plastic is forced into the mold under high pressure to form around the stamper. As the plastic cools, it hardens, taking on the patterns of the pits and lands found in the original master disk. The CD is inspected for such imperfections as dust particles, water bubbles, and warping. The CD is rejected if any imperfection is found.

11 The CD is transferred to a machine that punches a hole in its center. It is then coated with a thin layer of aluminum or silver using the process of vacuum deposition. The disk is put into a cold airless room. Then the metal coating is heated and evaporated and allowed to condense (turn into liquid) onto the chilled compact disk surface. Next, the disk is sealed with acrylic for protection. Finally, the disk is given a decorative label.

Packaging the game

12 All the components of the video game are transported to the packaging line. Each part of the game is placed in a preprinted cardboard box by automated machine or manually. The game boxes move by conveyor belt to a shrink-wrap machine that seals them in plastic. The sealed boxes are placed into cases and shipped for delivery.

Quality Control

The process of transferring the computer game program to a CD or a DVD must be done in a clean, dust-free environment. Dust particles, which are larger than the pits carved on the disk, can ruin them. Other visual inspections are done during the different steps of disk manufacture. Samples of the finished disk are also tested to make sure the video game program is working properly.

Other game components are also inspected to ensure they meet the required specifications. At the final manufacturing stage, samples of the complete product are checked to make sure all the components are present.

The Future

Video games have come a long way from their counterparts of the 1970s. Video games continue to improve, especially with the development of DVD technology, which promises to pack more information than CDs. Superior graphics and sound, numerous details, and sound effects have become the norm. Three-dimensional images and lifelike characters with music borrowed from star artists are the latest features of video games.

The number of video game players is growing, with more adults getting hooked on the games. Current figures show that nearly two of every five adult households in the United States own a video game system. The new consoles boast of built-in modems for surfing the Internet and online gaming. The video game industry predicts a future where many home video game systems will eventually be connected to the Internet.

For More Information

Books

Katz, Arnie, and Laura Yates. *Inside Electronic Game Design.* Rocklin, CA: Prima Publishing, 1996.

Olesky, Walter. *Video Game Designer.* New York, NY: The Rosen Publishing Group, Inc., 2000.

Web Sites

"The Exhibit of the True History of Video Games." *The Electronics Conservancy, Inc.* http://www.videotopia.com (accessed on July 22, 2002).

"GameSpy's 30 Most Influential People in Gaming." *GameSpy Industries.* http://www.gamespy.com/articles/march02/top30/127 (accessed on July 22, 2002).

Index

A

AbioCor Implantable Replacement Heart *3:* 35, 37, 38 (ill.)
Achard, Franz *3:* 90
Achilles tendon *1:* 195
Acoustic guitar *1:* 109 (ill.)
Adams, Thomas *2:* 58, 63
Advanced Photo System (APS) *3:* 212–213
Aerodynamics *1:* 3, 118
Aerosol insecticide *3:* 197
Agitation *1:* 159
Air bag *2:* 1–10, 1 (ill.), 2 (ill.)
Air bag components *2:* 4 (ill.)
Air bag manufacturing *2:* 6 (ill.), 7 (ill.), 8 (ill.), 9 (ill.)
Air conditioner *3:* **1–10,** 1 (ill.), 3 (ill.), 5 (ill.)
Airframe *1:* 120
Air-purifying respirator (APR) *3:* 123
Airtime *3:* 219
Alcoke, Charles *3:* 215
Aldrin, Edwin E. "Buzz," Jr. *3:* 259
Alignment *1:* 73
"All You Need Is Love" *3:* 226
AlliedSignal *1:* 49
Allison, Doug *2:* 18
Alloy *1:* 123, 258, 274
Amati, Andrea *2:* 279
American National Standards Institute *1:* 97
Amplification *1:* 107
Anaheim Stadium *1:* 212 (ill.)
Angioplasty *2:* 16, 17 (ill.)
Angle of incidence *1:* 55
Animation *3:* **11–20,** 14 (ill.), 15 (ill.), 16 (ill.), 18 (ill.)
Annatto *1:* 58

Annealization *1:* 77, 259; *2:* 42
Anodization *1:* 123
Antibiotic *3:* **21–29,** 21 (ill.), 26 (ill.), 27 (ill.)
Antioxidants *1:* 156; *2:* 251
Anti-smoking poster *3:* 86 (ill.)
Apothecary *1:* 220
APS. *See* Advanced Photo System (APS)
Aramid *1:* 121
Arbor *2:* 70
Arc lamps *1:* 145
Archer, Frederick *3:* 206
Archive *1:* 55
Argon *2:* 9, 169–172, 175
Armstrong, Neil A. *3:* 259, 269
Aromatherapy *2:* 201
Aromatics *2:* 194
Arrays *1:* 211
Artificial heart *3:* **30–40,** 30 (ill.)
Asaho, Kunji *2:* 129 (ill.)
Assembly lines *1:* 1, 4 (ill.), 6 (ill.), 7 (ill.), 9 (ill.), 33; *2:* 109, 125, 218, 222, 237, 239
Atari Company *3:* 278
Atlantis *3:* 259 (ill.)
Attenuation *1:* 172
Audio encoding *1:* 81
Auréole *3:* 145
Autoclaves *1:* 123, 267
Autogiros *1:* 117
Automobile *1:* 1–11, 149, 229; *2:* 1, 3, 4, 36, 46, 75, 109, 120, 173, 176, 243, 247, 270
Avobenzone *2:* 251
Axles *1:* 4
Aztecs *1:* 46

Italic type indicates Series number; **boldface** type indicates main entries featured in Series 3; (ill.) indicates photographs and illustrations.

B

Baer, Ralph *3:* 278
Baird, John Logie *3:* 270–271
Bale chambers *2:* 104
Baler pickup *2:* 104
Ball bearings *1:* 260
Balloon *2:* 11–17, 11 (ill.), 12 (ill.), 17 (ill.), 38, 40, 50
Balloon manufacturing *2:* 14 (ill.), 15 (ill.)
Ballpoint pen *3:* **41–48,** 41 (ill.), 43 (ill.), 45 (ill.), 46 (ill.)
Balm *1:* 155
Banbury, Fernely H. *2:* 227
Banbury mixer *2:* 227
Bar code scanner *1:* 12–19, 13 (ill.), 16 (ill.), 17 (ill.)
Bar codes *1:* 12–19, 12 (ill.)
Barnard, Christiaan *3:* 31
Basalt *1:* 201
Base notes *2:* 200
Baseball *1:* 20–26, 20 (ill.), 21 (ill.), 25 (ill.); *2:* 19
Baseball construction *1:* 24 (ill.)
Baseball glove *2:* 18–25, 18 (ill.), 19 (ill.), 23 (ill.), 25 (ill.)
Baseball glove manufacturing *2:* 20 (ill.), 24 (ill.)
Baseball player *1:* 22 (ill.)
Bean bag plush toy *3:* **49–59,** 49 (ill.)
Bean bag plush toy manufacturing *3:* 55 (ill.), 56 (ill.)
Beanie Babies *3:* 49–51, 50 (ill.), 53 (ill.), 57
Bearings *1:* 142
Beatles, The *3:* 226
Bedrock *1:* 214
Beeper *2:* 26–35, 26 (ill.), 27 (ill.), 33 (ill.), 34 (ill.)
Beeper manufacturing *2:* 29 (ill.), 31 (ill.), 32 (ill.)
Bees *1:* 18
Beeswax *2:* 57, 62
Bell, Alexander Graham *1:* 172
"Bends" *3:* 267
Benz, Carl *1:* 2
Bergman, Torbern *3:* 247
Berthollet, Claude-Louis *2:* 87
Beryl *1:* 89

Berzelius, Jons Jakob *3:* 270
Besson, Gustave Auguste *1:* 258
Bevels *1:* 92
BIC pens *3:* 43
Bich, Marcel *3:* 43
Bicycle *2:* 36–47, 36 (ill.), 39 (ill.), 40 (ill.)
Bicycle components *2:* 41 (ill.), 45 (ill.)
Bicycle Museum of America *2:* 38
Bidermann, Samuel *2:* 213
Bifocals *1:* 90
Billet press *2:* 188
Binding *1:* 37, 44 (ill.)
Binoculars *1:* 90
Bionic *1:* 115
Biotin *1:* 166
Biro, Georg *3:* 42
Biro, Laszlo *3:* 42
Black box *3:* **60–69,** 60 (ill.), 61 (ill.), 67 (ill.)
Black powder *2:* 86, 89–92
Blackton, James Stuart *3:* 12
Blanking die *1:* 77
Blanking punch *1:* 275
Blister pack *1:* 78
Blow molding *2:* 242–244, 252, 253
Blow torch *1:* 261
Blown rubber *1:* 194
Blue jeans *1:* 27–35, 28 (ill.), 29 (ill.), 274
Blue jeans manufacturing *1:* 31 (ill.), 32 (ill.), 33 (ill.)
Blueprints *1:* 42
Bluhmel, Friedreich *1:* 257
Bombarding *2:* 174–176
Bomber jacket *3:* 155 (ill.)
Boneshaker bicycle *2:* 38
Book *1:* 36–45, 36 (ill.), 39 (ill.)
Bookmatching *1:* 109
Bores *1:* 243
Box camera advertisement *3:* 208 (ill.)
Box tubular valve *1:* 257
Box-stitching *1:* 52
Bradham, Caleb *3:* 247–248
Brady, Matthew *2:* 207
Braider *2:* 52
Braille *1:* 18; *2:* 270
Brass *1:* 255, 256; *2:* 21, 90, 91
Braun, Ferdinand Karl *3:* 270
Brigandine armor *1:* 47 (ill.)
British thermal units (BTU) *3:* 1

Broth *1:* 63
Broyage *1:* 69, 70
Bubble gum *2:* 57–59, 63, 65
Budding, Edwin *1:* 137
Bulb-wall blackening *1:* 150
Bullet resistant vest. *See* Bulletproof vest
Bulletproof vest *1:* 46–55, 46 (ill.), 50 (ill.), 54 (ill.)
Bulletproof vest production *1:* 53 (ill.)
Bulletproof vest testing *1:* 48
Bungee cord *2:* 48–56, 48 (ill.), 49 (ill.)
Bungee cord manufacturing *2:* 52 (ill.), 53 (ill.)
Bungee jumping *2:* 48, 49 (ill.), 50, 51, 54, 55 (ill.), 56
Burn-in *2:* 127, 219
Bushnell, Nolan *3:* 278
Butting *2:* 42
Buttons *1:* 272
Bynema *1:* 49

C

Cacahuatl *1:* 63
Cadmium *1:* 77
Calcio *3:* 116
Calibration *1:* 245
Calotype *2:* 203; *3:* 205
Cam *1:* 75
Camera obscura *3:* 204
Camera-ready *1:* 44
Cameras *1:* 90; *2:* 120, 127, 129, 202–207, 210–212
Camp, Walter *3:* 118
Candler, Asa *3:* 255
Candy *1:* 71
Carbon *1:* 121, 145
Carbon black *1:* 247
Carbon rubber *1:* 194
Carbonated water *3:* 247
Carding *1:* 30
Carnauba *1:* 155
Carrier, Willis *3:* 2
Cartwright, Alexander *1:* 20
Carver, George Washington *2:* 178, 179 (ill.)
Casing in *1:* 38
Casting *1:* 122; *2:* 136

CAT. *See* Computerized Axial Tomography (CAT)
Catcher's mitt *2:* 18
Cathode ray tube (CRT) *3:* 273 (ill.)
Catsup. *See* Ketchup
Cavity *1:* 256
Cayley, George *1:* 116
CD. *See* Compact disc (CD)
Cedar *2:* 187–189
Cello *2:* 279, 282
Cello guitar *1:* 108
Cellular phone *2:* 33, 35, 82, 84
Cellulose *2:* 205, 207
Cels (celluloids) *3:* 19
Celsius, Anders *1:* 239
Cement lasting *1:* 194
Central note *2:* 200
Centrifugal pump *2:* 75
Centrifuge *1:* 225; *2:* 15, 61
Cereal *3:* 70–78, 70 (ill.), 71 (ill.), 76 (ill.)
Cereal manufacturing *3:* 73 (ill.), 74 (ill.)
Chain, Ernst *3:* 22
Chamois *1:* 192
Chandra X-ray Observatory *3:* 262
Changers *3:* 99
Charles, Jacques *2:* 11
Chassis *1:* 2
Cheese *1:* 56–62, 56 (ill.), 57 (ill.), 62 (ill.)
Cheese making *1:* 59 (ill.), 61 (ill.)
Chewing gum *2:* 57–65, 57 (ill.), 58 (ill.), 62 (ill.), 64 (ill.), 89, 191, 193, 194
Chewing gum manufacturing *2:* 60 (ill.), 61 (ill.), 63 (ill.)
Chicle *2:* 58–60, 63
Chip shooter *2:* 30
Chocalatl *1:* 63
Chocolate *1:* 63–72, 63 (ill.), 64 (ill.), 200; *2:* 100
Chocolate candy *1:* 67 (ill.)
Chocolate candy production *1:* 70 (ill.)
Chordophone *1:* 107
Christerson, Tom *3:* 38
Chromization *1:* 77
Chu, Grace *2:* 96
Cierva, Juan de la *1:* 117
Cigarette *3:* 79–88, 79 (ill.), 80 (ill.), 83 (ill.), 86 (ill.)

Italic type indicates Series number; **boldface** type indicates main entries featured in Series 3; (ill.) indicates photographs and illustrations.

INDEX **xi**

Italic type indicates Series number; **boldface** type indicates main entries featured in Series 3; (ill.) indicates photographs and illustrations.

INDEX **xiii**

Ford, Henry *1:* 1–2, 3 (ill.)
Forging *1:* 122
Formaldehyde *1:* 165
Fortrel EcoSpun *2:* 246, 247
Fortune cookie *2:* 96–101, 96 (ill.), 97 (ill.), 98 (ill.)
Fortune cookie manufacturing *2:* 99 (ill.), 100 (ill.)
Fractional distillation *2:* 169
Fragrances *2:* 193–196, 199–201
Frankincense *2:* 57, 194
Franklin, Benjamin *1:* 80 (ill.)
Freeblowing *1:* 124
French Harmless Hair Dye Company *3:* 145
Freon *2:* 2
Fresnel lens *2:* 265
Frets *1:* 107; *2:* 282
Friction inertial welding *2:* 6
Fuel cell *3:* 140
Functional testing *2:* 140
Fuselage *1:* 120

G

Galileo Galilei *1:* 238
Galleys *1:* 39
Galoshes *1:* 273
Galvanometer *1:* 210
Gama, Vasco da *1:* 219
Game Boy *3:* 279–280
Gas additives *3:* 139 (ill.)
Gas mask *3:* 123–131, 123 (ill.), 124 (ill.), 125 (ill.), 127 (ill.)
Gas mask assembly *3:* 129 (ill.)
Gas mask manufacturing *3:* 128 (ill.)
Gas mask testing *3:* 130 (ill.)
Gas station *3:* 135 (ill.)
Gasoline *3:* 132–141, 132 (ill.)
Geissler, Johann Heinrich Wilhelm *2:* 169
Gelatin *2:* 203, 204, 207, 209, 210
Gemini 3: 258
General Electric (GE) *2:* 131, 270
General Motors (GM) *2:* 51, 120, 124
Generator *1:* 94
Genovese *1:* 27
George Eastman House *2:* 205
Gerbach, A. *1:* 274

Germanium *1:* 14
Gershwin, George *2:* 216
Gertie the Dinosaur 3: 12, 13 (ill.)
Gibbon, John H. *3:* 31–32
Ginned cotton *1:* 30
Glass *1:* 84, 89; *2:* 67, 71, 162, 163, 169–176, 196, 198, 199, 203, 204, 241, 242, 247, 266
Glassblowing *1:* 241
Glue *1:* 229
Godwin, Linda *3:* 259 (ill.)
Gold *1:* 83; *2:* 206, 236
Goldenrod *1:* 41
Goldmark, Peter *3:* 271
Goldsmith, Michael *3:* 171
Golitsyn, Boris *1:* 210
Goodhue, Lyle *3:* 197
Goodyear, Charles *1:* 191, 247; *2:* 226
Gore closure *1:* 193
Gorie, John *3:* 2
Gortex *3:* 263
Graham, Sylvester *3:* 70
Granola *3:* 70
Granulator *1:* 227
GrapeNuts *3:* 71
Graphite *2:* 93, 186–191
Gravity Pleasure Road *3:* 215
Gravity Pleasure Switchback Railway *3:* 215
Gravure *1:* 42, 185
Gray, Laman *3:* 37
Gray, Thomas *1:* 210
Gridiron design *3:* 118
Grinding *1:* 94
Gruentzig, Andreas *2:* 16
Guarneri, Bartolomeo Giuseppe *2:* 279
Guitar *1:* 107–114, 107 (ill.), 109 (ill.), 113 (ill.); *2:* 279
Guitar manufacturing *1:* 111 (ill.)
Gum. *See* Chewing gum
Gumballs *2:* 62
Gunpowder *2:* 2, 86, 87, 89
Gutenberg, Johann *1:* 36

H

H. J. Heinz Company *2:* 162, 168
Hagiwara, Makoto *2:* 97
Hahn, Max *2:* 131

Italic type indicates Series number; **boldface** type indicates main entries featured in Series 3; (ill.) indicates photographs and illustrations.

INDEX **XV**

Ionization chamber smoke detectors 2: 233

IPLVAS *See* HeartMate Implantable Pneumatic Left Ventricular Assist System (IPLVAS)

Iron oxide *1:* 98

ISO. *See* International Standards Organization (ISO)

J

Jarvik, Robert *3:* 33 (ill.)

Jarvik-7 3: 31–32, 33 (ill.)

Jarvik-2000 Flowmaker 3: 39

Jenkins, Charles Francis *3:* 270

Jenny airmail stamps *1:* 189 (ill.)

Jersey (material) *2:* 256

Jet engine *2:* 131–141, 131 (ill.), 133 (ill.), 134 (ill.), 135 (ill.), 136 (ill.), 140 (ill.)

Jet engine manufacturing *2:* 137 (ill.), 138 (ill.), 139 (ill.)

Joyner, Fred *1:* 230

Judson, Whitcomb L. *1:* 272

Jung, George *2:* 97

K

Kantrowitz, Adrian *3:* 32, 39

Karman, Theodore von *1:* 117

Karp, Haskell *3:* 32

Kellogg, John Harvey *3:* 70

Kellogg's Corn Flakes *3:* 70

Kelly, Charlie *2:* 38, 40

Kelvin, Lord *1:* 239

Keratometers *2:* 67

Ketchup *2:* 161–168, 161 (ill.), 164 (ill.)

Ketchup manufacturing *2:* 162 (ill.), 165 (ill.), 166 (ill.), 167 (ill.)

Kevlar *1:* 48, 51, 173; *2:* 114, 133, 137; *3:* 263

Kevlar production *1:* 51 (ill.)

Kircher, Athanasius *3:* 11

Kodak *2:* 204 (ill.), 205, 206 (ill.), 212

Kolff, Willem *3:* 32

Krazy Kat 3: 12

Krypton *2:* 169

Kumax *1:* 49

Kwolek, Stephanie *1:* 48

L

Laboratory incubator *1:* 206

Lacquer *1:* 262

Laid paper *1:* 184

Landrum, Ed *2:* 214 (ill.)

Lands *1:* 83

Laps. *See* Lens laps

Lappers *2:* 70

Laser cutting *1:* 84

Laser drilling *2:* 137

Laser welding *2:* 6

Lasers *1:* 12, 80, 172; *2:* 6, 32, 70, 107, 123, 127, 137

Lassiter, John *3:* 14

Latex *1:* 247; *2:* 11–17, 50, 57–60, 227

Lathes *2:* 273

Lavassor, Emile *1:* 2

Lawn mower *1:* 137–144, 137 (ill.), 138 (ill.), 141 (ill.), 143 (ill.)

LCD. *See* Liquid crystal display (LCD)

Lead glass *2:* 171

Leap pad *1:* 94

Leather *1:* 191; *2:* 20–22, 24, 25, 41, 102, 111, 114, 194

Leather jacket 3: 153–161, 153 (ill.), 155 (ill.), 160 (ill.)

Leather jacket assembly *3:* 159 (ill.)

Leather jacket design *3:* 158 (ill.)

Left ventricular assist device (LVAD) *3:* 30, 32, 35

Legumes *2:* 178

Lenoir, Etienne *1:* 2

Lenses *1:* 14

Lens laps *1:* 94

Lensometers *1:* 93, 95 (ill.)

Leonardo da Vinci *1:* 116; *2:* 36

Letterpress *1:* 42

Light bulb *1:* 145–153, 145 (ill.), 148 (ill.), 152 (ill.); *2:* 176, 266

Light bulb manufacturing *1:* 151 (ill.)

Light detection system *1:* 14

Light-emitting diode (LED) *1:* 240, 267

Light-sensitive paper *1:* 210

Lindbergh, Charles *3:* 61

Linnaeus, Carolus *1:* 65

Italic type indicates Series number; **boldface** type indicates main entries featured in Series 3; (ill.) indicates photographs and illustrations.

INDEX **xvii**

M

MIDI. *See* Musical instrument digital interface (MIDI)

Miller, John A. *3:* 223

Milne, John *1:* 210

Mind Eraser (roller coaster) *3:* 222 (ill.)

Mineral tanning *3:* 156

Mineral water *3:* 246–247

Miners *1:* 28 (ill.)

Minkoff, Larry *3:* 171

Mir 3: 259 (ill.), 262

Mirrors *1:* 14

MIT. *See* Massachusetts Institute of Technology (MIT)

Mitt *2:* 18, 25

Model A automobile *1:* 1

Model T automobile *1:* 1, 3 (ill.), 4 (ill.)

Modified Chemical Vapor Deposition (MCVD) *1:* 175, 176

Modulus *2:* 230

Molten sodium silicate *1:* 121

Monasterio violin *2:* 280 (ill.)

Monopoly *1:* 219

Monroe, William *2:* 187

Montgolfier, Jacques *2:* 11

Montgolfier, Joseph *2:* 11

Moonwalks *3:* 259

Morgan, Garrett A. *2:* 270; *3:* 123–124, 126

Morse, Samuel F. B. *2:* 207

Mortar *1:* 200

Mosquito *3:* 195 (ill.)

Mosquito breeding ground *3:* 196 (ill.)

Mosquito repellent *3:* **195–203**

Mosquito repellent manufacturing *3:* 200 (ill.), 201 (ill.)

Mosquito repellent testing *3:* 202 (ill.)

Mountain bikes *2:* 38, 39

Movie projector *3:* 12

MRI. *See* Magnetic Resonance Imaging (MRI)

Mullen, Ernest *2:* 67

Multimode *1:* 173

Multiple-effect evaporation *1:* 225

Murrie, Bruce *3:* 163

Museum of Electronics *2:* 30

Museum of Neon Art *2:* 171

Museums *2:* 30, 38, 171, 205

Musical Instrument Digital Interface (MIDI) *2:* 216, 218, 221, 222

Musk *2:* 195, 200

Mutt and Jeff 3: 12

Mycenaeans *1:* 46

Mylar *1:* 101; *2:* 12; *3:* 258, 263

Myrrh *2:* 193, 194

Mystic Color Lab *2:* 211

N

Nail polish *1:* 164–171, 164 (ill.), 165 (ill.), 169 (ill.); *2:* 208

Nail polish manufacturing *1:* 167 (ill.), 168 (ill.)

Napoleon Bonaparte *2:* 87, 196

NASA. *See* National Aeronautics and Space Administration (NASA)

National Aeronautics and Space Administration (NASA) *3:* 258

National Collegiate Athletic Association (NCAA) *3:* 118

National Food Processors Association *1:* 227

National Football League (NFL) *3:* 118

National Institute of Justice (NIJ) *1:* 54

National Institute of Law Enforcement and Criminal Justice *1:* 49

National Institute of Occupational Safety and Health (NIOSH) *3:* 131

National Institute of Standards and Technology *1:* 240

National Optical Association *1:* 97

National Transportation Safety Board (NTSB) *3:* 63

National Transportation Safety Board investigator *3:* 64 (ill.)

NCAA. *See* National Collegiate Athletic Association (NCAA)

Negatives *1:* 41

Neon art *2:* 171

Neon lamp *1:* 147

Neon sign *2:* 169–177, 169 (ill.), 170 (ill.), 172 (ill.)

Neon sign manufacturing *2:* 173 (ill.), 174 (ill.), 175 (ill.)

Neoprene *2:* 51, 81, 123, 266

Neumann Tackified Glove Company *2:* 25

New York Stock Exchange *3:* 2

Newton, Isaac *2:* 132

Newton's third law of motion *2:* 131

Italic type indicates Series number; **boldface** type indicates main entries featured in Series 3; (ill.) indicates photographs and illustrations.

INDEX **xix**

Perinet, Francois *1:* 257
Perkin, William *2:* 195
Perlman, Itzhak *2:* 287, 288 (ill.)
Permanent hair color *3:* 145
Perry, Thomas *2:* 226
Persians *1:* 46
"Persistence of vision" *3:* 274
PET. *See* Polyethylene terephthalate (PET)
Peter, Daniel *1:* 66; *3:* 163
Petroleum-based products *1:* 2
Petronas Twin Towers *3:* 235, 236 (ill.), 244
Pharmacist *3:* 24 (ill.)
Phenakistoscope *3:* 12
Philately *1:* 185
Phonographs *1:* 80
Phosphor tagging *1:* 183
Photo sensors *1:* 84
Photodetectors *1:* 14
Photodiodes *1:* 14
Photoelectric smoke detectors *2:* 233
Photograph *3:* **204–213**, 204 (ill.)
Photograph development *3:* 209, 210 (ill.)
Photograph manufacturing *3:* 211–212
Photograph materials *3:* 207–209
Photographic film *2:* 202–212, 202 (ill.), 203 (ill.), 206 (ill.)
Photographic film manufacturing *2:* 208 (ill.), 209 (ill.)
Photography *2:* 202–205, 207, 212
Photometers *2:* 181
Photoresist *1:* 84
Photosynthesis *1:* 220
Piano. *See* Player piano
Piano action *2:* 213
Picasso, Paloma *1:* 156
Pierce, John R. *3:* 226
Pietz, John *2:* 1
Piezoelectricity *1:* 266
Pigments *1:* 155, 166; *2:* 12, 13, 14, 188, 191, 227, 237, 254, 286
Pigskin *3:* 118
Pills *1:* 21
Pipeline *3:* 140
Pitch *1:* 260
Pits *1:* 83
Pixels *1:* 106
Pixilation *3:* 13
Planktons *3:* 132

Plantain trees *1:* 63
Plasma *1:* 140
Plasma screen *3:* 276
Plastic creep *2:* 244
Plasticizers *1:* 164
Plateau, Joseph *3:* 12
Plating *1:* 75, 76
Player piano *2:* 213–224, 213 (ill.), 214 (ill.), 219 (ill.), 223 (ill.)
Player piano (disc-driven) *2:* 217 (ill.), 220 (ill.)
Playstation *3:* 285 (ill.)
Plimpton, James *2:* 111
Plucking *1:* 107
Point size *1:* 39
Point-of-sale scanners *1:* 12
Polaroid film *2:* 207, 210
Polishing *1:* 94
Polycarbonate *1:* 91, 93
Polycarbonate sheeting *1:* 121
Polyester *2:* 12, 241, 247, 256
Polyethylene *1:* 173; *2:* 59, 241, 243, 247
Polyethylene terephthalate (PET) *2:* 184, 241–245, 247
Polymers *1:* 230, 247; *2:* 65, 68, 72, 73, 114, 242, 243, 245, 247
Polymerization *1:* 50; *2:* 242, 243, 245
Polyurethane *1:* 194; *2:* 114
Polyvinyl chloride (PVC) *1:* 101
Poly-para-phenylene terephthalamide *1:* 48
Pong *3:* 278
Pop-up books *1:* 38
Porcelain *1:* 149
Porsche *1:* 5 (ill.)
Post, Charles William *3:* 71
Post Toasties *3:* 71
Postage stamp *1:* 181–190, 181 (ill.), 182 (ill.), 183 (ill.), 189 (ill.)
Poulsen, Valdemar *1:* 98
Powder metallurgy *2:* 134, 136, 139
Power reel mowers *1:* 139
Pratt & Whitney *2:* 141
Pre-preg ply *1:* 123
Presley, Elvis *1:* 184 (ill.)
Press cakes *1:* 71
Press proofs *1:* 43
Press-Ewing seismographs *1:* 211
Priestley, Joseph *2:* 225; *3:* 247

Italic type indicates Series number; **boldface** type indicates main entries featured in Series 3; (ill.) indicates photographs and illustrations.

INDEX **xxi**

S

Italic type indicates Series number; **boldface** type indicates main entries featured in Series 3; (ill.) indicates photographs and illustrations.

INDEX **xxiii**

Terrain *1:* 195
Thenard, Louis-Jacques *3:* 145
Thermal cracking *3:* 138
Thermometer *1:* 238–245, 238 (ill.), 239 (ill.)
Thermometer manufacturing *1:* 243 (ill.), 244 (ill.)
Thermoplastic *2:* 252
Thermoscopes *1:* 238
Thompson, LaMarcus *3:* 215
Thorax *1:* 18
Tiemann, Ferdinand *2:* 195
Tillotson, Neil *2:* 11
Time lock *1:* 74
Tire *1:* 49, 246–254, 246 (ill.), 247 (ill.), 248 (ill.), 253 (ill.); *2:* 38, 40, 45, 46, 108, 140
Tire manufacturing *1:* 251 (ill.), 252 (ill.)
Titanium *1:* 48, 121; *2:* 40, 41, 89, 114, 133, 134, 136, 137, 251
Thomson, William. *See* Kelvin, Lord
Tobacco growing *3:* 82 (ill.)
Tobacco manufacturing *3:* 83 (ill.)
Toilet water. *See* Eau de toilette
Tomatillos *1:* 200
Tomatoes *2:* 161, 163, 165, 168
Top note *2:* 200
Torque *1:* 120
Touhy, Kevin *2:* 67
Toy Story *3:* 14
Tractor *1:* 139; *2:* 84, 102, 104, 106
Traffic signal *2:* 264–270, 264 (ill.), 265 (ill.), 267 (ill.), 268 (ill.); *3:* 126
Traffic signal components *2:* 269 (ill.)
Transformers *2:* 172
Transmissions *1:* 5
Travers, Morris William *2:* 169
Trumpet *1:* 255–263, 255 (ill.), 256 (ill.), 263 (ill.)
Trumpet components *1:* 261 (ill.)
Trumpet manufacturing *1:* 260 (ill.)
Tsung, David *2:* 96
Tungsten *1:* 147
Turbine blades *2:* 133, 136, 137, 139
Turbine discs *2:* 136, 139
Turbofan engines *2:* 132, 135
Turbojet engines *2:* 132
Turboprop engines *2:* 132
Turning machines *2:* 273
Tush tags *3:* 51, 54

Twaron *1:* 49
Two-dimensional bar code *1:* 19
Tyers, Robert John *2:* 111
Typeface style *1:* 39
Typesetters *1:* 37 (ill.)
Typesetting *1:* 38, 39, 40 (ill.)

U

Ultrasonic testing *1:* 142
Ultraviolet (UV) radiation *2:* 68, 69, 248, 249, 251, 253, 254, 258
Umbrella *2:* 271–278, 271 (ill.), 273 (ill.), 276 (ill.)
Umbrella components *2:* 274 (ill.)
Umbrella manufacturing *2:* 275 (ill.)
Underwater Locator Beacon (ULB) *3:* 64–65
Underwriters Laboratories (UL) *2:* 176, 223
Unicycle *2:* 37 (ill.)
U. S. Environmental Protection Agency (EPA) *1:* 242; *3:* 140
U. S. Food and Drug Administration (FDA) *1:* 97; *2:* 179, 180, 184, 249, 251; *3:* 151
U. S. Post Office *2:* 225
UV. *See* Ultraviolet (UV) radiation
UVA. *See* Ultraviolet (UV) radiation
UVB. *See* Ultraviolet (UV) radiation
UVC. *See* Ultraviolet (UV) radiation

V

Vacuum deposition *1:* 86
Vacuum evaporation *1:* 224
Vacuum packing *2:* 184
Van Wijnen, Wim *2:* 46
Vapor deposition method *1:* 173, 175
Vatelot, Etienne *2:* 287 (ill.)
Vaults *1:* 74
Vegetable tanning *3:* 156
Vehicle Identification Number (VIN) *1:* 10
Velcro *1:* 49; *2:* 114–116
Velocipede *2:* 38
Veneer *1:* 229

Italic type indicates Series number; **boldface** type indicates main entries featured in Series 3; (ill.) indicates photographs and illustrations.

INDEX **XXV**

Vertical fiber drawing *1:* 176

VGA Flight Recorder 3: 62

Video game *3:* 277–287, 277 (ill.), 279 (ill.), 281 (ill.), 283 (ill.)

VIN. *See* Vehicle Identification Number (VIN)

Viol *2:* 279, 282

Viola *2:* 279, 282

Violin *2:* 279–289, 279 (ill.), 280 (ill.), 281 (ill.), 287 (ill.), 288 (ill.)

Violin components *2:* 284 (ill.)

Viscosity *1:* 105, 234

Von Drais, Baron Karl *2:* 36

Von Linde, Carl Paul Gottfried *2:* 170

Vulcanization *1:* 247; *2:* 14, 226–228

Vulcanized rubber *1:* 191

W

Waite, Charles G. *2:* 18

Waksman, Selman *3:* 22

Walker, Lewis *1:* 272

Wand scanners *1:* 12

Warner, H. Ty *3:* 49–51

Warp *1:* 30, 31

Watch *1:* 264–271, 264 (ill.), 266 (ill.), 271 (ill.); *2:* 35

Watch assembly *1:* 269 (ill.)

Water blanching *2:* 182

Waterman, Lewis Edison *3:* 42

Waterproof mascara *3:* 180

Wax *2:* 58, 62, 70, 136, 139, 162, 187, 188, 191

"Weathermaker" *3:* 3

Wedgwood, Thomas *3:* 205

Weft *1:* 31

Weld *1:* 6

Welt *1:* 193

Wet plate *3:* 206

Whittle, Frank *2:* 131

Wichterle, Otto *2:* 68, 69

Williams, T. L. *3:* 179

Wilson Football Factory *3:* 121–122

Windmills *1:* 117

Windows *1:* 14

Windshields *1:* 8; *2:* 8

Wirewrapping machines *1:* 250

Woggel, Michael *1:* 257

Work, Bertram G. *1:* 273

World-Wide Standardized Seismograph Network (WWSSN) *1:* 210

Wright, Orville *3:* 60

Wright, Wilbur *3:* 60

Wunderlich, Carl *1:* 240

WWSSN. *See* World-Wide Standardized Seismograph Network (WWSSN)

Wyeth, N. C. *2:* 242

Wyeth, Nathaniel C. *2:* 241

X

X-ray *2:* 210

X-ray videography *1:* 252

Xenon *2:* 169

Y

Yeager, Chuck *2:* 141

Yeast *1:* 68

Z

Zahn, Johann *3:* 204

Zamak *1:* 75

Zeiss, Carl *2:* 67

Zinc *1:* 75; *2:* 251

Zipper *1:* 272–280, 272 (ill.), 273 (ill.), 279 (ill.)

Zipper components *1:* 275 (ill.)

Zipper manufacturing *1:* 276 (ill.), 277 (ill.)

Zoetrope *3:* 12

Zworykin, Vladimir *3:* 271